"*Consider Your Counsel* sheds humble evaluation and contir book to the newest and most se... to join me in revisiting it often."

Eliza Huie, Author of *Raising Kids in a Screen-Saturated World*

"Throughout this book, Bob's heart for others shines through. Never the stern or austere judge, he serves as a loving and patient guide. This brief book should be required for all counselors, new and old alike."

Jonathan D. Holmes, Executive Director, Fieldstone Counseling; Pastor of Counseling, Parkside Church

"Bob Kellemen reminds us that using the Bible alone is not biblical counseling. We must care about *how* we use the Bible and *how* we relate to counselees. Both novice and seasoned biblical counselors can appreciate the balanced insights in this book as we consider our counsel for the glory of God."

Lilly Park, Associate Professor, Southwestern Baptist Theological Seminary

"When I read books on counseling, I measure them by the chapters that speak to my need to be a better counselor. *Consider Your Counsel* by Bob Kellemen helps me in all ten chapters. There is so much good in this book for anyone who wants to be better at helping others!"

Charles D. Hodges Jr., Practicing Family Physician in Indianapolis, Indiana; executive director, Vision of Hope, Lafayette, Indiana

"Bob Kellemen's work in *Consider Your Counsel* is profoundly scriptural and transformative. It is an essential guidebook for the new and seasoned biblical counselor."

Shannon Kay McCoy, ACBC; biblical counseling director, Valley Center Community Church; council member, Biblical Counseling Coalition

"Supported with Scripture while also offering wisdom from historical examples of faithful soul care, this is a book I want to get into the hands of my students as they move from the theory to the practice of biblical counseling."

Jim Newheiser, Director of the Christian Counseling Program, RTS Charlotte; executive director IBCC; author of *Money, Debt, and Finances*

"Prevention and correction. These are two marvelous benefits that come from reading *Consider Your Counsel*. The biblical counseling movement will be well served by this excellent resource for generations to come."

C. W. Solomon, Executive Director, The Biblical Counseling Coalition

"Any counselor, no matter how much experience they have, will be edified with the reading of Bob's perception of common mistakes in counseling. Please read it, consider it, and grow in personal holiness and ministry faithfulness."

Alexandre "Sacha" Mendes, Pastor; board of directors of the Biblical Counseling Coalition; director at ABCB (Brazilian Association of Biblical Counseling)

"*Consider Your Counsel* is comprehensive in that it highlights different pitfalls to avoid, provides helpful self-assessments, and provides necessary advice for correction if needed. It is also succinct and extremely valuable to both the novice and seasoned counselor. I am excited to add it to the required readings list for my team of counselors."

Ben Marshall, Pastor of Counseling, Canyon Hills Community Church, Bothel, Washington; ACBC and IABC certified biblical counselor

"Bob Kellemen is a counselor of counselors, and this book is his equipping workshop. More than a list of common mistakes, this is a foundational philosophy of counseling in an accessible and concise form. If it is said so often that it has become cliché, the saying is true in this case: this is a book all counselors need to read!"

David R. Dunham, Pastor of Counseling & Discipleship, Cornerstone Baptist Church

"In *Consider Your Counsel,* Dr. Kellemen continues his consistent emphasis on Christlike, incarnational, personal ministry. This work on compassionate soul care ministry is a stimulating challenge to veteran counselors as well as needed training for new biblical counselors."

Brent Aucoin, Pastor of Seminary and Soul Care Ministry, Faith Church, Lafayette, Indiana

"*Consider Your Counsel* is a gift to the church by casting a vision for compassionate, comprehensive, and communal care that reflects the God of all comfort and our Good Shepherd. This work will benefit every church leader and member as we seek to bear one another's burdens."

Robert K. Cheong, Pastor of Care, Sojourn Church Midtown; executive director, Gospel Care Ministries

CONSIDER YOUR COUNSEL

ADDRESSING TEN MISTAKES IN OUR BIBLICAL COUNSELING

Bob Kellemen

New
Growth
Press

newgrowthpress.com

New Growth Press, Greensboro, NC 27404
newgrowthpress.com
Copyright © 2021 by Bob Kellemen

Cover Design: Faceout Books, faceoutstudio.com
Interior Design and Typesetting: Gretchen Logterman

ISBN: 978-1-64507-145-7 (Print)
ISBN: 978-1-64507-146-4 (eBook)

Library of Congress Cataloging-in-Publication Data

Names: Kellemen, Robert W., author.
Title: Consider your counsel : addressing ten mistakes in our Biblical
  counseling / by Bob Kellemen.
Description: Greensboro, NC : New Growth Press, [2021] | Includes
  bibliographical references. | Summary: "Drawing from more than three
  decades of counseling supervision, author Bob Kellemen shares ten
  counseling missteps he has noticed in himself and others"-- Provided by
  publisher.
Identifiers: LCCN 2020054956 (print) | LCCN 2020054957 (ebook) | ISBN
  9781645071457 (trade paperback) | ISBN 9781645071464 (ebook)
Subjects: LCSH: Counseling--Religious aspects--Christianity. | Pastoral
  counseling.
Classification: LCC BR115.C69 K43 2021 (print) | LCC BR115.C69 (ebook) |
  DDC 253.5--dc23
LC record available at https://lccn.loc.gov/2020054956
LC ebook record available at https://lccn.loc.gov/2020054957

Printed in the United States of America

28 27 26 25 24 23 22 21   1 2 3 4 5

Contents

ACKNOWLEDGMENTS

AS YOU'LL read in the introduction, *Consider Your Counsel* was birthed by a question asked by biblical counseling students I supervise. So, it seems only fitting that I dedicate this book to an array of students I've supervised over the past thirty-plus years. Though I can't name you because I would never have the space, you know who you are. Thank you each for your commitment to learning and growing as biblical counselors. Your humble openness to feedback, your deep desire to mature as a counselor, and your loving passion for ministering God's Word to God's people are so encouraging to me.

In a similar spirit, I'd also like to dedicate *Consider Your Counsel* to you—my readers. You wouldn't be reading this book unless you shared that same desire to keep maturing as a biblical counselor. I pray that the reading and applying of this book will stretch and strengthen you just as the writing of it has done for me.

And I surely want to thank the team at New Growth Press. I've been privileged to work with a lot of publishers. Working with New Growth Press is more than working with a publisher—it's working with friends who care about their work, about my writing, and about me. Thank you Barbara, Ruth, Irene, Cheryl, Karen, Mark, and the rest of the team—the rest of the "family."

INTRODUCTION
A WORD FROM BOB

THIS BOOK began when several biblical counseling students who had been under my supervision asked my thoughts on common themes, threads, and patterns I detected as a counseling supervisor. They were specific: "We're not asking about all the 'good stuff' we do as biblical counselors. We're interested in the consistent areas where you sense a need for growth." Because it's a passion of mine to encourage biblical counselors who are looking for ways to grow, their question intrigued me. And, since I'm a collator of patterns, their request sent me back to my supervisory notes—resulting in this book.

ENCOURAGEMENT, NOT CRITIQUE

My only hesitation in collating these ten mistakes into book form is that I do *not* want to foster a negative perception of the modern biblical counseling movement. I'm a big fan of biblical counseling and biblical counselors. *I'm* a biblical counselor. I've invested over thirty years into providing biblical counseling, equipping biblical counselors, and supervising biblical counselors. It was one of the greatest joys of my ministry life to be the founding executive director of the Biblical Counseling Coalition. The vast majority of the content I've written in more than 2,500 blog posts, more than 150 published articles, and more than twenty books and booklets focuses on a positive presentation of biblical counseling and Christian living.

That said, there's something healthy and humble about a movement self-assessing, self-critiquing, and self-correcting—biblically, wisely, collaboratively, and graciously. Indeed, the modern biblical counseling movement was launched with the concept of confronting out of concern for change. And biblical counseling is well known for self-counsel and self-confrontation. So it would be unusual for us as biblical counselors not to consider our counseling individually and collaboratively.

Rather than focusing on critique, this book highlights tendencies I've noticed in the thousands of biblical counselors I've trained and the hundreds of biblical counselors I've supervised over the past thirty years. These include laypeople in four churches, pastors, counselors, Bible college students, and seminary students in over a dozen schools (as a professor and as an adjunct/visiting professor). My supervisees also include experienced counselors and mature pastors who have requested additional counseling supervision. I poured over my supervision notes asking, *What patterns, themes, and threads of blind spots do I detect in rookie and veteran biblical counselors*—myself included—*from which we could learn and grow?*

Although I've been providing biblical counseling for thirty-five years, I have made these mistakes. Even "seasoned" biblical counselors can benefit from a course correction. We are wise to regularly self-assess and to have others speak into our practice of biblical counseling. My heart behind sharing these ten observations is to encourage all of us to continue to deepen and develop as biblical counselors. Biblical counselors are well known for emphasizing progressive sanctification—ongoing growth in Christ. We can think of this book as part of that iron-sharpening-iron process of progressively growing together as biblical counselors.

DRAWING POSITIVES OUT OF NEGATIVES

When I supervise counselors, I spend a good deal of time affirming the positives I see. For instance, "That was great how you interacted there. Keep doing more of that!" or "Wow! That was amazing how you connected Scripture to life there. What biblical insights led you to pursue that helpful direction?"

Even if I detect weaknesses or "mistakes," my aim in discussing them is to help counselors-in-training to mature. For instance, "Your interaction there seems a tad off track in this specific way. . . . Let's talk about what might have been going on there. What way of thinking about counseling might have led to that interaction? And let's ponder what you—and I—could learn from this."

That's the plan in addressing these ten common counseling mistakes—growing together. You'll note that I'll spend less time highlighting the mistake and most of my time devoted to describing a biblical alternative and what a more biblical approach might look like. Think of this book as *supervision by writing*. My chief desire in crafting this material is that it would be an encouraging refresher tool for us as biblical counselors.

A final word before we start addressing these common mistakes: this list does not attempt to say everything that could be said about the essence of helpful biblical counseling. For more on biblical counseling theology, see *Gospel-Centered Counseling*.[1] For more on biblical counseling methodology, see *Gospel Conversations*.[2]

Let's begin learning together—from our mistakes. Let's keep learning and growing into more mature biblical counselors who speak and live God's truth in love.

MISTAKE #1:

WE ELEVATE DATA COLLECTION
ABOVE SOUL CONNECTION

THE MODERN biblical counseling movement does a fine job at data collection. We've been accurately taught to heed biblical wisdom about listening before speaking, such as, "If one gives an answer before he hears, it is his folly and shame" (Proverbs 18:13). "Know this, my beloved brothers: let every person be quick to hear, slow to speak, slow to anger" (James 1:19).

We wisely use our Personal Information Forms to collect pages of information and reams of data about our counselee. We learn important information about their unique situation, their family background, the suffering they have endured, the besetting sin they are battling, their relationship to Christ, and so much more. All of this is very good, healthy, helpful, and wise. Let's continue to collect data.

SOUL CONNECTION IS THEOLOGICAL

And yet . . . people are not car engines we fix by reading a mechanic's manual. People are not computers we treat by reading the operator's guide.

People are image bearers of our relational God who exists in eternal, Triune community of Father, Son, and Holy Spirit (Genesis 1:26–28). The Word was and is eternally with God in intimate face-to-face communion (John 1:1–18). Adam—while in perfect communion in a perfect garden with a perfect God—still was alone and needing the companionship of Eve (Genesis 2:18). We are relational.

Soul connection in counseling is theological because God designed us to relate intimately to him and to one another. Counseling that stops at data collection is *not biblical* counseling.

Data collection without soul connection can end up treating image bearers like lab specimens to be analyzed and dissected. It can become aloof, impersonal, and uncaring—and even un-Christlike.

SOUL CONNECTION IS BIBLICAL: PAUL MODELS IT CONSISTENTLY

So what are we to do instead of impersonal data collection? We are to pursue personal connection. Sometimes this means stopping in the middle of collecting background information and praying because you can tell the person is overwhelmed by what they're sharing. Other times it means weeping with counselees as they weep. Primarily it emphasizes relational involvement where you enter the unique soul and the personal story of your counselee—human being to human being.

During supervision I've observed the opposite of this many times. A counselee moves from intellectually sharing information to emotionally breaking down. The counselor then either continues to ask factual questions or begins teaching. As the supervisor, I'll interject myself into the live counseling to encourage the counselor to put down their pen and notes, stop teaching, and *be relationally present with their counselee in that moment*.

This is what Paul did in his ministry with people—with relational image bearers. Ponder just a few examples from Paul's relational ministry.

- *Paul models sharing Scripture and soul.*

   "So, being affectionately desirous of you, we were ready to share with you not only the gospel of God but also

our own selves, because you had become very dear to us"
(1 Thessalonians 2:8).

- *Paul models the compassionate care of personal ministry.*

"My little children, for whom I am again in the anguish of
childbirth until Christ is formed in you!" (Galatians 4:19).

- *Paul models the family and relational nature of personal
  ministry.*

"But we were gentle among you, like a nursing mother
taking care of her own children. . . . For you know
how, like a father with his children, we exhorted each one
of you and encouraged you and charged you to walk in
a manner worthy of God" (1 Thessalonians 2:7, 11–12).

- *Paul models the passion and closeness of personal ministry.*

"For this I toil, struggling with all his energy that he
powerfully works within me. For I want you to know how
great a struggle I have for you" (Colossians 1:29–2:1).

- *Paul models heart and soul relationship in the personal ministry of the Word.*

"We have spoken freely to you, Corinthians, and opened
wide our hearts to you. We are not withholding our
affection from you, but you are withholding yours from
us. As a fair exchange—I speak as to my children—open
wide your hearts also" (2 Corinthians 6:11–13 NIV).

SOUL CONNECTION IS HISTORICAL: CHURCH HISTORY MODELS IT CONSISTENTLY

Octavia Albert knew something about suffering and about comforting others in their suffering. Albert was a formerly enslaved,
college-educated African-American pastor's wife living in Louisiana. In the 1870s, she ministered to many formerly enslaved men

and women by recording their stories of suffering. One of those individuals was Charlotte Brooks. Of Brooks, Albert writes, "It was in the fall of 1879 that I met Charlotte Brooks. . . . I have *spent hours with her listening to her telling of her sad life of bondage* in the cane-fields of Louisiana" (emphasis added).[1]

We would be miles ahead in our biblical counseling if we would follow Albert's model of *spending hours listening to sad stories*. Rather than simply collecting data, we enter the situation and soul of another person as we listen compassionately to their story.

As we listen to our counselees' earthly stories, we need to empathize with them in their story. Empathy is not some secular Trojan horse that seeks to sneak extra-biblical concepts into our biblical counseling. Empathy is a biblical word and a scriptural concept. Think of the word *em-pathos*—to enter the pathos or the passion of another, to allow another person's agony to become our agony, to weep with those who weep (Romans 12:15).

Notice how Octavia Albert allowed Charlotte Brooks's agony to become her own. "Poor Charlotte Brooks! I can never forget how her eyes were filled with tears when she would speak of all her children: "Gone, and no one to care for me!"[2]

Like Octavia Albert, as we listen and collect data, we connect soul to soul, human being to human being, image bearer to image bearer, sufferer to sufferer. Not only must we feel what another person feels, we need to express and communicate that we "get it," we feel it, we hurt too. Consider how Octavia Albert does this with Aunt Charlotte. "Aunt Charlotte, my heart throbs with sympathy, and my eyes are filled with tears, whenever I hear you tell of the trials of yourself and others."[3]

What Brooks modeled in 1879, the church has long called "compassionate commiseration." *Co-passion*: to share the passionate feelings of another. *Co-misery*: to partner in the misery of our friend.

SOUL CONNECTION IS SCRIPTURAL: GOD COMMANDS IT OF US

Paul commands every member of the body of Christ to "speak the truth in love" (Ephesians 4:15). We are to embody truth in the context of a sacrificial, intimate, caring, and connected relationship. Our words of truth and challenge to our counselees can only be received and trusted as a foundation of genuine love and care is being established.

The Holy Spirit sovereignly combined the members of the body of Christ so "that there may be no division in the body, but that the members may have the same care for one another. If one member suffers, all suffer together; if one member is honored, all rejoice together" (1 Corinthians 12:25–26).

Paul prays for us that our "love may abound more and more, with knowledge and all discernment" (Philippians 1:9). The heartbeat of Scripture always beats to the rhythm of *truth and love*, *Scripture and soul*, and *wisdom and relationship*. As biblical counselors, we seek to be Christlike counselors—full of *both* grace and truth. We grow in this relational competency as we wisely and carefully combine comprehensive data collection with compassionate soul connection.

SUPERVISION TAKEAWAYS

With counselees, after a long and intense session I'll often say, "We talked about a lot of important matters today. Of everything we shared, let's each take a minute or two to jot down a couple of major takeaways." These often end up becoming our collaboratively created "homework" assignments for that counselee. Though this book is like supervision in writing, you and I can't cocreate supervision homework assignments. However, I would encourage you to ponder after each chapter what the biggest takeaways are for you as a biblical counselor. I'll seek to do the same at the end of each chapter by collating four counselor self-assessment questions. Here's our first set of questions:

ASSESSING OUR BIBLICAL COUNSELING

1. In our biblical counseling, would people say of us, "I feel like a soul to be heard, known, understood, and cared

about"? Or, would they say of us, "I feel like a specimen to be probed, dissected, examined, and diagnosed"?

2. In our biblical counseling, would people say of us, "She loves me like a tender, gentle mother. He loves me like an encouraging, comforting father"?

3. Would the people we counsel say of us, "They share Scripture and soul. They model intimacy and intensity. They relate like a family and a community"?

4. In our biblical counseling, how richly and compassionately are we empathizing with the situation and soul of our brothers and sisters in Christ?

MISTAKE #2:

WE SHARE GOD'S ETERNAL STORY BEFORE LISTENING TO PEOPLE'S EARTHLY STORY

IN THE previous chapter, we noted from Proverbs 18:13 and James 1:19 the importance of listening. Every biblical counselor believes in this critical skill, yet I've found that many of us use an abbreviated listening method that I call *listen and pounce!*

AVOID THE "SHALLOW CONCORDANCE APPROACH" TO COUNSELING

We listen, but at times we fall into the trap of racing through the listening process. We're basically listening for key words that we think give us permission to interrupt our counselee and interject our "wisdom" before we've truly heard the speaker.

A wife might be ten minutes into sharing her story in counseling when she slips out the word *fear*. Something internally nudges our mind and we think, *She said "fear." I know a verse for fear!* Then we race to preach at her 2 Timothy 1:6–7, focusing on not having a spirit of timidity or fear, but a spirit of power, love, and wisdom as she clings to Christ. We use a "concordance approach" to Scripture that makes the Bible a shallow answer book rather than the redemptive gospel story that it is.

There are a multitude of possibilities for what might be going on in this woman's situation and soul. For example, if we really kept listening to this young wife, we might learn that she is not experiencing sinful fear but realistic, legitimate fear at the hands of an abusive husband. By prematurely preaching 2 Timothy 1:6–7 to her, we may well shame her into thinking the issue is her problem—she's not submissive enough to her husband and she's not trusting God enough. A slowed-down, unhurried approach to hearing her full story would enable us to accurately understand her situation and compassionately care for her soul.

REMEMBER TWO PICTURES: USE TWO EARS; PIVOT YOUR FEET

If we're not to simply listen for words to pounce on, what are we to do? We listen to the *whole person's whole story* as we listen together to God's whole redemptive story.

When I'm teaching this to counselors, I'll say, "Now, hands off your Surface Pro, eyes up, please look at me." I'll continue, as I cup one ear. "With one ear, we're always listening patiently, compassionately, and wisely to the person's earthly story of suffering, pain, struggle, sin, sanctification." Then I'll cup my other ear. "Simultaneously, we're always listening—together—to Christ's eternal story of the cross: redemption, resurrection, reign, and return."

Then I'll switch metaphors. "Now, watch my feet. With one foot, we enter deeply and personally into our counselee's story, situation, and soul. With the other foot, we pivot into and journey together to Christ's story of redemptive hope. Our calling is to step into and move between two worlds, between two stories as we help our counselees see how Christ's redemptive story intersects and invades our counselee's troubling story."

Recently I was counseling a young man who had experienced repeated relational disappointment. As we talked and I drew out what was going on at a deeper level, it became clear that the worst pain was not just the breach in his relationships, but his sense of aloneness. "It seems like no one understands. No one really hears me. They try to fix me. They give me counsel to try to fix the relationships—and I appreciate all of that. But they're not stopping to hear how isolated I feel." After probing further about his sense of aloneness (because I wanted to be sure he was *heard*), I asked, "Is there any passage or person in Scripture you identify with who has felt this same sense of not being heard, of being alone in sorrow?" His eyes lit up. "Two people. One man. One woman. Job, throughout the whole book, and especially in Job 3, seemed to be screaming how unheard he felt! And then Hagar, in Genesis 16 was unheard but then was so comforted that God heard and saw her."

We then spent the rest of our time that meeting exploring those passages. First, my young friend found comfort in being able to identify with Job in his isolation. Then he found hope—gospel hope—as he took his aloneness and not being heard to the God of Hagar who hears and sees our misery. Rather than racing my friend to a quick answer, we slowly journeyed together, taking his unique soul question to God's ever-relevant Word.

Pastor and author Dietrich Bonhoeffer powerfully captures the importance of this dual listening to the person's story and to God's story.

> For Christians, pastoral care differs essentially from preaching in that here the task of listening is joined to the task of speaking the Word. There is also a kind of listening *with half an ear* that presumes already to know what the other person has to say. This *impatient, inattentive listening* really despises the other Christian and finally is only *waiting to get a chance to speak and thus to get rid of the other*. This sort of listening is no fulfillment of our task. But Christians have forgotten that the ministry of listening has been entrusted to them by the one who is indeed *the Great Listener* and in whose work they are to participate. We should listen with the ears of God, so that we can speak the Word of God. (emphases added)[1]

PRACTICE LINGERING LISTENING INSTEAD OF LISTEN AND POUNCE

Moving between these two worlds, these two stories—our counselee's story and God's story—requires *lingering listening* where we listen well and wisely to the person's *situation* and to their *soul*. This is vital for a number of reasons; I'll highlight two of them.

First, we earn the right to explore Scripture with another person by deeply caring about the person's situation and soul. It's similar to evangelism. It's the rare person who wants to hear us share about Christ if they don't know us, or if they don't know that we care about them.

In 1 Thessalonians 2, Paul models the vital connection between the message, the messenger, and the person receiving the message. Paul doesn't just dispense facts. He shares Scripture and soul as he relates to them as a brother, mother, father, child/orphan, and mentor.

Second, we learn the right Scriptures to explore by richly understanding our friend's situation and soul. Biblical counseling is *not* one problem→one verse→one solution→every person. It is *not* a one-size-fits-all formula.

Biblical counseling is the *personal* ministry of the Word where we explore together the *specific* biblical passages and scriptural principles that best relate to this *particular* person. Biblical counseling is God's wisdom for life in a broken world—a fallen, messy world that requires depth of insight, not shallow platitudes.

CONSIDER "THE BIBLICAL COUNSELOR'S PRAYER"

To discern the best counsel for a particular counselee in their unique situation, we pray what I call "The Biblical Counselor's Prayer" from Philippians 1:9–11.

> And it is my prayer that your love may abound more and more, with knowledge and all discernment, so that you may approve what is excellent, and so be pure and blameless for the day of Christ, filled with the fruit of righteousness that comes through Jesus Christ, to the glory and praise of God.

This passage and prayer teaches us that rather than one-size-fits-all advice, we seek person-specific wisdom from above as we counsel. As a unique image bearer sits across from us, we pray,

"Father, what *particular* aspect of hope in Christ does this *unique* friend's soul need in his or her *specific* situation?"

To connect God's story and people's story, we must listen, not prattle, as Bonhoeffer again reminds us.

> Many people are looking for an ear that will listen. They do not find it among Christians *because Christians are talking where they should be listening.* But he who can no longer listen to his brother will soon no longer be listening to God either; he will be doing nothing but prattle in the presence of God too. One who cannot *listen long and patiently* will presently be *talking beside the point* and never really be speaking to others. Anyone who thinks that his time is too valuable to spend keeping quiet will eventually have no time for God and his brother, but only for himself and his own follies. (emphases added)[2]

LEARN FROM THE HOLY SPIRIT

Here's our tendency when we hear a problem: we race in with Romans 8:28 and preach how God works all things together for good. Great verse. Powerful. And our desire to share it is often motivated by compassion for the person and by confidence in God's Word.

However, scroll your eyes up two verses to Romans 8:26. Note that before the discussion of how God works all things together for good, we learn that the Spirit *groans together* with suffering saints. The Spirit knowing us and suffering with us is the context for the Spirit highlighting God's affectionate sovereignty over us. That's a powerful personal ministry principle: *groaning before guiding.*

Do we groan with others—identify with their suffering—before we offer guidance? Do we feel before we fix? Do we understand before we speak?

Yes, speak truth in love. But first, love. Know. Listen. Relate.
Care. Connect. Comfort. Groan. Counsel like the Holy Spirit
who groans as he guides.

LEARN FROM CHRIST

We're told in John 2:24–25 that Jesus did not entrust himself
to anyone because he knew what was in every person. In the
next two chapters of John, this "people wisdom" guided Jesus to
minister very differently to two very different people—because
he knew them and listened carefully to each of them.

In one corner was Nicodemus, the male, Jewish religious
leader. In the other corner was the female, irreligious Samaritan
woman. As we read John 3 and 4, we detect particular aspects
of gospel hope that Jesus focused on as he ministered to these
two very unique souls with two very different and specific life
situations. To Nicodemus, he talked about theology applied to
life—the kingdom of God, being born again, and the resurrection.
Jesus illustrated his message from the Old Testament. He pierced
Nicodemus's proud heart with words about absolute dependence.
To the Samaritan woman, Jesus connected life to theology—
physical thirsts to spiritual thirsts. He illustrated his message with
common elements from her life—including her need for God in
her suffering and sin.

Jesus understood each individual and *tailored his message and
his method* to their distinctive story. Jesus does not model one-
size-fits-all counsel. Our Divine Counselor models person-specific
biblical counseling that listens to people's earthly story as the foundation for connecting their story to God's eternal story.

ASSESSING OUR BIBLICAL COUNSELING

1. In our biblical counseling, do we listen and pounce—
   preaching *at* people and doing so unwisely and prematurely? Or do we practice lingering listening to their

whole story—taking the time to understand the person's situation and soul?

2. As biblical counselors, do we see our calling as journeying together with our counselees so that they can grasp how Christ's redemptive story intersects and invades their troubling story?

3. As biblical counselors, do we follow the model of the Holy Spirit—the Divine Counselor within us—who groans before and as he guides?

4. As biblical counselors, do we follow the model of Jesus—the Wonderful Counselor—by seeking to understand each individual and by tailoring our exploration of Scripture to their distinctive situation, story, and soul?[3]

- Lingering before
   listening

MISTAKE #3:

WE TALK *AT* COUNSELEES RATHER THAN EXPLORING SCRIPTURE *WITH* COUNSELEES

AS I supervise biblical counselors, I've noticed a common pattern of practicing counseling as if it is biblical *teaching*—rather than biblical *counseling*. Yes, teaching is a component of counseling. But counseling is not identical to teaching.

Typically, the bulk of our counselor training comes via lecture. No matter how many times the instructor says, "Though I'm lecturing right now, please don't think counseling equals lecturing," students still perceive a one-to-one correlation between lecturing and counseling.

Counseling, or the *personal* ministry of the Word, is different from preaching/teaching, or the *public* ministry of the Word. While the public ministry of the Word is powerful and absolutely essential in our Christian lives, we should not think of biblical counseling as preaching or teaching to an audience of one. The beauty and benefit of the personal ministry of the Word is the give-and-take relationship that occurs as we relate God's truth specifically to a person's unique situation, soul, and story.

COLLABORATIVE BIBLICAL COUNSELING

People often ask me whether biblical counseling is directive or nondirective. I typically respond that I prefer a third category: *collaborative*.

In purely *directive* counseling, the counselor is the expert lecturer who talks *at* and teaches truth *to* the counselee. The counselee at times is almost perceived to be inferior to the counselor. In purely *nondirective* counseling, the counselee is the expert on his or her own life. The counselor's role is simply to draw out wisdom from within the counselee.

Throughout church history a third method of care has been prominent, as noted by church historians William A. Clebsch and Charles R. Jaekle, in their classic book *Pastoral Care in Historical Perspective*. In historic pastoral counseling, the Bible is the guide and the pastor journeys with the counselee as both seek to relate the wisdom of the Word to the counselee's life.[1] This is collaborative biblical counseling. The pastor-counselor is typically still more knowledgeable about the Word, but that knowledge is not used in a "one-up" way as an expert talking at or talking down to a novice. Instead, that knowledge is a resource used for joint exploration of God's character and wisdom as revealed in the sufficient Scriptures.

THE DIFFERENCE BETWEEN GIVING A FISH OR TEACHING TO FISH THE SCRIPTURES

Picture the contrast between directive counseling and collaborative counseling like this:

- Teaching/Telling Scripture→Give a Person a Fish→ Make a Student of Yourself
- Exploring Scripture Together→Teach a Person to Fish→ Make a Disciple of Christ

I've supervised many counselors whose model or approach is to "give a fish"—to talk at and teach to a counselee in an attempt to spoon-feed all the answers to their situation. They tend to have a one-size-fits-all model for counseling, where they take anyone and everyone through the same six or eight-session Bible study. It's often a good Bible study. Yet this counselor often says with some exasperation, "I'm not sure why my counselee isn't growing. Why isn't the truth changing how they handle their life situation?"

There are a couple of important answers to that honest question. First, as we saw in our discussion in chapter 2, this directive approach to the Bible is too generic. The counselor is often not relating God's story to the *unique* situation, soul, and story of their *specific* counselee.

Second, any change that may occur is likely to be so focused on one area of difficulty that the counselee will have a hard time applying Scripture to other areas of struggle. They have been given a fish but not taught how to fish—they have been given a type of solution for today's problems but not equipping in biblical wisdom for tomorrow's new challenges. They have been told how to overcome one life issue, but they have not been discipled in how to search and apply the Scriptures to grow in grace in all of life.

As biblical counselors, we use our understanding of Scripture not just to "give a fish." Instead, we train counselees *how to fish the Scriptures*—how to apply God's truth to their life and relationships. The counselee becomes a disciple of Christ the Divine Counselor instead of merely being a student of a human teacher. The counselee should be discipled to do ongoing *self-counsel* by learning how to turn to God's Word for wisdom for life.

TRIALOGUES

To move from giving a fish to equipping counselees to fish the Scriptures, let's examine the concept of *trialogues*.[2] A monologue is when I talk to you, teach you, or preach to you. I speak to you. A dialogue is when you and I engage in a back-and-forth, give-and-take conversation. We speak to each other. A trialogue is when three people are included in our gospel conversation: the counselor, the counselee, and the Divine Counselor through God's Spirit and God's Word. Together the counselor and counselee listen to God's Word, discerning how to apply truth to life.

In trialoguing, we take our theological understanding (God's story), listen to our counselee's story (situation and soul), and then

interact together in ways that invite them to ponder how God's
story interprets, intersects, and invades their story.

Trialogues require that counselors have a Spirit-led dependence upon God, which results in a Philippians 1:9–11 discernment of scriptural passages and biblical wisdom principles that
best relate to the counselee's life (see chapter 2). Trialogues also
require counselors to know biblical passages so well that they are
able to guide a counselee through *understanding the text in context
and applying it to the counselee's personal context.* As an example,
consider the trialogues below from 2 Samuel 13. (Notice the biblical preparation needed by the counselor to explore the depth and
richness of this passage with a counselee).

BIBLICAL SAMPLER OF EXPLORING SCRIPTURES TOGETHER IN TRIALOGUES

What does exploring Scriptures together look like? Imagine that
you're counseling Ashley. It's the day after her twin sons' eleventh
birthday. With tears streaming down her face, Ashley shares that
twenty-five years earlier, not long after her own eleventh birthday, a relative began sexually abusing her.[3]

Imagine that you've met several times with Ashley and her husband (Nate) to hear Ashley's story and to empathize with her suffering. Then you begin interacting with Ashley about 2 Samuel 13
and the rape of Tamar by her half-brother Amnon. Consider a
sampler of the trialogues you could engage in with Ashley. First,
let's explore in the following points some general trialogues about
the passage.

- "Ashley, as you read Tamar's story, what is similar in what
  happened to her compared to what you experienced?
  What is different in Tamar's story from what happened
  to you?"
- "Ashley, as we read about Tamar's response in verses 12–21,
  what is similar and what is different in her response from
  your response?"

Because the Bible is real and raw, this passage allows Ashley and you to explore aspects of Tamar's rape that are potentially comparable to the abuse Ashley experienced. The fact that the Bible talks about these experiences can help free Ashley to talk about her experiences.

- "Ashley, as we read about the setup in 13:5–10, what feelings does that stir in you? How were you set up by your abuser?"
- "What do you feel when you read Amnon saying he 'loved' his sister?"
- "The Bible is raw and honest. We're told in 13:12–16 that Amnon forced Tamar, refused to listen to her, overpowered her, and raped her. What is it like for you to read those words? How do those descriptions compare to your abuse?"
- "What do you think it was like for Tamar to experience her brother's brutality? Hatred? Betrayal? How does her experience compare to yours?"
- "Amnon later acted as if Tamar was the guilty party—he treated her like a 'thing' and like a dangerous woman (13:15–17). Did you experience this victimizing of the victim? Being treated like a non-person? Like the guilty party? What was this like for you?"
- "Tamar's beauty, femininity, and servant's heart are all used against her (13:1–2, 5–11). How do you think this impacted Tamar? How would this impact you?"

The Bible is not only real about the external abuse; it realistically depicts the internal soul struggles. Now you can explore heart struggles with Ashley in a trialogue manner, allowing Scripture to introduce a variety of themes for consideration. For example,

- "In 13:12–16, we see Tamar's battles with powerlessness and voicelessness. How do her struggles compare to yours?"

- "We're told that Tamar struggled with feelings of disgrace, desolation, and shame (13:13, 20). Have you battled any of these feelings? Other feelings? What are you doing with those feelings? How do you see yourself?"
- "Family words like 'sister' and 'brother' are used repeatedly in this passage—highlighting the pain of incestuous abuse. What do you feel when you read those words?"
- "Tamar grieves deeply. She tore her richly ornamented robe, put ashes on her head, and wept aloud (13:18–19). How does Tamar's grief response compare to yours? Have you given yourself permission to grieve like Tamar? What would it be like for you to lament to God?"

The Bible also depicts realistically how other family members often revictimize the victim. You can explore these common dynamics with Ashley.

- "Tamar's other brother, Absalom, responds in a horribly hurtful way by telling her to be quiet and not to take this thing to heart (13:20–22). Who has responded to you in similarly hurtful ways? What has that felt like?"
- "Tamar's father, King David, was angry but inactive (13:21). Who has responded to you in a similarly hurtful way? What did that feel like?"
- "David grieves the death of Amnon (13:39), but we're never told he grieves the rape of Tamar. Honestly, that makes me furious. What feelings does that bring up for you?"

God's Word never leaves us without hope, even in a passage like 2 Samuel 13 that focuses so much on Amnon's sin and Tamar's suffering. So you can explore hope-giving, God-facing trialogues like these with Ashley.

- "Given the culture of her day, it's remarkable that Tamar somehow found the strength to speak forcefully about the foolish, wicked nature of Amnon's sin (13:12–13). Where do you think Tamar found the courage to overcome her feelings of powerlessness and voicelessness and speak out like this? Through Christ's strength, how are you finding the strength to do the same?"

- "In 2 Samuel 13, we find an inspired account of a wicked event. God speaks through the narrator and through Tamar to voice God's view of this abuse. God calls sexual abuse wicked and foolish (13:12–13). How does it impact you to know that God is on the side of the abused and stands against your abuser?"

- "Just two chapters earlier, we read of David's great sin (2 Samuel 11). In this section of Scripture, how is God directing our gaze to a focus on our fallen condition? How is God directing our gaze to our desperate need for the Greater David—for Jesus?"

Biblical counseling is discipleship—we equip counselees in how to turn to God and God's Word for wisdom for life in their broken world. Through collaborative biblical counseling where we explore Scripture with our counselees, we enlighten them to experience how richly relevant God's Word is for all of life. We empower counselees to be their own best biblical counselor—to do biblical self-counsel 24/7.

ASSESSING OUR BIBLICAL COUNSELING

1. Is our biblical counseling more directive (counselor as expert teller), more nondirective (counselees as experts about their own life), or more collaborative (counselor and counselee guided together by God's Word)?

2. As biblical counselors, which of the following is truer of our focus?

   a. Teaching/Telling Scripture→Give a Person a Fish→ Make a Student of Yourself

    b. Exploring Scripture Together→Teach a Person to
    Fish→Make a Disciple of Christ

3. As biblical counselors, do we practice monologue counseling, dialogue counseling, or <u>trialogue counseling—where there are three people in our gospel conversation: the counselor, the counselee, and the Divine Counselor</u> through God's Spirit and God's Word? Do we listen together to God's Word, discerning collaboratively how to apply truth to life?

4. As biblical counselors, how could the 2 Samuel 13 sample trialogues impact our counseling practice, our counseling process, our counselor-counselee relationship, and our counselee's life?

MISTAKE #4:

WE TARGET SIN BUT DIMINISH SUFFERING

IN THE 1960s, British Christian psychiatrist Frank Lake noted that, "pastoral care is defective unless it can deal thoroughly *both with the evils we have suffered as well as with the sins we have committed*" (emphasis added).[1] The modern biblical counseling movement has made tremendous strides in the past several decades in addressing both sin *and* suffering. Most biblical counselors now helpfully look at Christian counselees through the lens of *saints* who face *suffering* and battle against *sin* on their *sanctification* journey of growth in Christlikeness.

And yet, as I supervise counselors—whether experienced pastors or laypeople who are rookie counselors-in-training—I continue to detect a pattern of viewing fellow Christians predominantly through the grid of depravity and thinking of counseling primarily as "spotting idols of the heart."

This one-dimensional lens can cause great harm. Recently while supervising a counselor during a live counseling session, I observed as the counselor listened as his male counselee talked about his responses to several life losses and ministry difficulties. Quite quickly, the counselor moved into idols of the heart, sharing, "It sounds to me like you have an idol of the heart of comfort and ease. Where can we look in Scripture to see how God wants you to repent of this heart idolatry?" Now, this was one possible thread to *eventually* address, but there seemed to me to be little factual evidence to draw this conclusion. Plus, the timing seemed wrong. I could sense the shame and confusion that this mature believer—who had served the Lord vocationally for decades—was experiencing in this moment. So I stepped in. We then began to co-counsel and explore the situation more fully—coming to understand that this brother was experiencing legitimate grief. This man's sorrow over his suffering was the appropriate initial place to focus, not some assumed "idol of comfort."

Follow-up counseling between this counselor and counselee led to some breakthrough times where the counselee was able to deeply and richly lament to the Father of compassion and the God of all comfort. Interestingly, both the counselor and the counselee have since expressed how much more powerful their counseling ministry has become because they are now able to address issues of both sin and suffering.

Frank Lake describes what happens to counselees when counselors minimize suffering: "But, like Job, they complain of the comforters whose one-track minds have considered only the seriousness of sin, and not the gravity of grinding affliction."[2] If we fail to carefully self-assess our biblical counseling, we can become guilty of one-track "sin spotting." Instead, let's be comprehensive, compassionate biblical counselors who address the gravity of grinding affliction.

ADDRESSING SUFFERING ALSO ADDRESSES SIN

When I talk about addressing both sin and suffering, some people will raise the question, "Are you saying that our greatest problem is our brokenness and victimization, not our personal sinfulness?" That's an important question that deserves careful consideration. What I am saying is summarized in the following points.

1. Our greatest problem is sin.
2. Our greatest need is Christ as our Savior from sin.
3. Sin reveals itself in our sinning against God *and* against one another.
4. When we sin against one another, we cause each other great suffering and pain.

5. The Trinity models compassion, comfort, and empathy to those in suffering (we'll address this in chapter 5).
6. The Scriptures command Christians to suffer with, weep with, empathize with, comfort, care for, and encourage one another in suffering (we'll also explore this in chapter 5).
7. When we address suffering we are addressing sin—sin's cosmic and personal impact.

Christ's victory over sin was not only individual and personal but also corporate and cosmic. Christ died to dethrone sin. Christ died to defeat every vestige of sin, to obliterate every effect of sin—individual, personal, corporate, and cosmic—including death, suffering, tears, sorrow, mourning, crying, and pain.

That's why John shares twice in Revelation the blessed promise that, "He will wipe away every tear from their eyes, and death shall be no more, neither shall there be mourning, nor crying, nor pain anymore, for the former things have passed away" (Revelation 21:4; see also Revelation 7:17). Christ died to defeat every enemy and every evil, including the devil who holds the power of death (Hebrews 2:14–15) and the last enemy—suffering and death (1 Corinthians 15:25–26).

When we invite people to come to us with their grief and suffering, rather than ignoring or minimizing sin, we are actually emphasizing and addressing the deep impact of sin. That's what Frank Lake meant when he said we must deal thoroughly both with the evils we have suffered and with the sins we have committed. Biblical counselors recognize that not all suffering is due to personal sin (compare Job 1–2 and John 9). Therefore, not all counseling focuses upon confrontation of the sins we have committed.

BIBLICAL COUNSELORS ARE *PARAKALETIC* COUNSELORS FOR THE SUFFERER

The Greek word *parakaletic* pictures a person called alongside to help another person in need. The Bible uses variants of this term more than 110 times in the New Testament. By comparison, it uses forms of the Greek word *nouthetic* (conveying the idea of confronting sin out of concern for change) eleven times in the New Testament. The Bible calls us to be both *parakaletic* comfort-ers of the suffering and *nouthetic* care-fronters of those battling besetting sins—biblical counselors do not target sin and diminish suffering.

In John 14, John uses *parakaletic* when he describes the Holy Spirit as our Comforter/Counselor. He is our encouragement Counselor, called not simply alongside but inside us to help and comfort us after Jesus ascends to heaven. Likewise, we are to follow the Spirit's *parakaletic* model. In 2 Corinthians 1:3–7, Paul uses various forms of the root word *parakaletic* ten times in five verses to describe the calling of the body of Christ to come alongside, empathize with, comfort, and encourage one another during times of affliction. God calls each of us to be *parakaletic* biblical counsel-ors—biblical soul caregivers to those facing suffering and longing for biblical healing hope.

We live in a fallen world and it often falls on us. Biblical counselors gladly assume the role of encouragers to help a friend crushed by the weight of the world. As the Good Samaritan paused his journey and bloodied himself to care for a stranger's suffering body, so soul caregivers move near to enter the mess and muck of a friend's suffering soul. When we respond like this to suffering counselees, we can become to them a small picture of the infinite care of Christ. As we explore in the next chapter, our care points them to Christ's care.

God calls us to develop the competency to be *parakaletic* comforters who minister to people suffering under the gravity of grinding affliction. *Comfort* is a powerful word in English as well as Greek. In English, it highlights *co-fortitude*—the idea that we are fortified when we stand together; we are strengthened when others weep with us and grieve with us (Romans 12:15). Shared sorrow is endurable sorrow.

We *compassionately identify with people in pain.* We reject the shallow pretense that denies suffering. Like Jeremiah, we lament. Like Paul, we groan for home. We're out of the nest. East of Eden. We're not home yet. We join our hurting spiritual friend in admitting that life is hard.

PARAKALETIC BIBLICAL COUNSELORS ARE CHRIST-CENTERED

We also insist that *God is good.* Therefore, we don't direct people to ourselves. We shun their becoming dependent upon us. Instead, we redirect people to Christ and the body of Christ. We point suffering friends to their suffering Savior (Hebrews 4:14–16). We remind them what a Friend they have in Jesus.

What is the focus of our *parakaletic* biblical counseling for suffering? We sometimes miss the profound biblical truth that when we minister to a suffering person, our goal is not only to care for them but also to help them grow in Christ. We need to link our ministry to the suffering with the ministry of sanctification—growth in grace. Satan wants sufferers to think that when life is bad, God is bad too. We journey with sufferers as they seek a gospel-centered perspective that *even when life is bad, God is good.* We help suffering friends to find God even when they can't find relief. They become more like Christ as they cling humbly to Christ.

ASSESSING OUR BIBLICAL COUNSELING

1. Is our biblical counseling defective because it deals thoroughly with the sins we have committed but not with the evils we have suffered?
2. As biblical counselors, do we sometimes have a one-track mind that considers the seriousness of sin but neglects the gravity of grinding affliction?

3. Do we see ourselves as *parakaletic* biblical counselors—
   biblical soul caregivers who comfort, encourage, and
   compassionately care for those facing suffering?
4. As biblical counselors, do we compassionately identify
   with people in pain and direct them to Christ and the
   body of Christ for comfort and healing hope?

MISTAKE #5:
WE FAIL TO FOLLOW THE TRINITY'S MODEL OF COMFORTING CARE

IN THE previous chapter, we explored how our counseling sometimes focuses on sin but downplays suffering. In our desire to root out sin, we can neglect our calling to comfort people in their suffering, grief, loss, pain, and hurt. If we're not careful, we can end up counseling like Job's miserable counselors whose one-track minds spotted sin instead of comforting Job in his suffering. The motivation behind this focus on sin is often a desire to be like God in his holiness. We don't want to wink at sin. We want to speak the truth.

However, in our desire to counsel like God, we must recall that God is a God of *holy love*, of *truth and grace*, of *righteousness and mercy*, of *confrontation of sin and compassion for suffering*. As biblical counselors, in addition to confronting sin, we must follow the Trinity's model of comforting the suffering.

The most important thing about us as biblical counselors is maintaining a biblical view of God. The same holy, transcendent Sovereign Lord who comes with power to rule and reward in righteousness (Isaiah 40:10) is also our loving, immanent Comforting Counselor who, "will tend his flock like a shepherd; he will gather the lambs in his arms; he will carry them in his bosom, and gently lead those that are with young" (Isaiah 40:11). The Trinity's comforting care for the suffering is the model and motivation behind biblical counselors providing the *parakaletic* care we highlighted in chapter 4.

LET'S COUNSEL LIKE THE FATHER OF COMPASSION AND THE GOD OF ALL COMFORT

In the last chapter, we noted that Paul uses the Greek word for "comfort" ten times in 2 Corinthians 1:3–7. Do you think comfort may be the theme of these verses? He begins developing his theme by presenting a crystal clear image of God: "Blessed be the God and Father of our Lord Jesus Christ, the Father of mercies and God of all comfort, who comforts us in all our affliction, so that we may be able to comfort those who are in any affliction, with the comfort with which we ourselves are comforted by God" (2 Corinthians 1:3–4). All comfort is ultimately sourced in God. The flip side of that is to say that worldly comfort—comfort not sourced in God—is ultimately empty, vain, hollow comfort.

Counsel like Our Compassionate Father

The Greek word for "mercies" ("compassion" in the NIV) means to feel another person's agony. People in Paul's day used the word to signify *sympathetic lament*. Isaiah 63:9 tells us that in all Israel's distress, God too was distressed. God laments our pain; God aches when we ache; he weeps when we weep. He is the Father of compassion.

Is this our image of God when life is bad? In our suffering, do we see God as our Father who sympathetically laments with us?

Is this our functional image of God as biblical counselors? When suffering friends and counselees come to us, do we sympathetically lament with them? This involves their pain becoming our pain—we feel their inner suffering as if it was our own. Practically, I've expressed this to counselees by writing a psalm of lament on their behalf—expressing what I feel as I seek to grasp their pain. Often this has given them permission to grieve, and it has opened up their heart to craft their own lament psalm.

Counsel like Our Comforting Father

God is the God of all comfort. The word for "comfort" pictures God caring for us and fortifying us. He gives us his strength to endure. Paul and others used the word *comfort* to picture

- a lawyer advocating for a client,
- a mother wrapping her arms of protection around her child,
- a solider standing back-to-back with a comrade in danger.

In the midst of our suffering, is this our image of God? In our suffering, do we see God as our Advocate, as our Protector, as our Ally? Is this our functional image of God as biblical counselors? When suffering friends and counselees come to us, do they experience us as their caring advocate, as their concerned protector, as their empathetic ally?

LET'S COUNSEL LIKE JESUS, OUR SYMPATHETIC HIGH PRIEST
Jesus is the Wonderful Counselor (Isaiah 9:6). And yet our Counselor is the man of sorrows, acquainted with grief (Isaiah 53:3).

The New Testament picture further develops this Old Testament image. Jesus is our sympathetic High Priest.

> Since then we have a great high priest who has passed through the heavens, Jesus, the Son of God, let us hold fast our confession. For we do not have a high priest who is unable to sympathize with our weaknesses, but one who in every respect has been tempted as we are, yet without sin. Let us then with confidence draw near to the throne of grace, that we may receive mercy and find grace to help in time of need. (Hebrews 4:14–16)

Jesus identifies with us—empathizing and sympathizing with us. And as we turn to him, we receive grace, mercy, and help in our weakness, neediness, suffering, and sinfulness.

Jesus shared in our humanity *so that* he might be a merciful and faithful High Priest.

> Therefore he had to be made like his brothers in every respect, so that he might become a merciful and faithful high priest in the service of God, to make propitiation for the sins of the people. For because he himself has

suffered when tempted, he is able to help those who are being tempted. (Hebrews 2:17–18)

What Hebrews describes, Jesus models in his ministry. We think of John 11 and tend to focus on verse 35: "Jesus wept." A moving verse, no doubt, and certainly indicative of Jesus as a man of sorrows and as our sympathetic High Priest, but we sometimes miss the verses that precede and follow John 11:35.

When Jesus saw her weeping, and the Jews who had come with her also weeping, he was deeply moved in his spirit and greatly troubled. (John 11:33)

As we weep, do we see Jesus deeply moved and troubled over our suffering?

So the Jews said, "See how he loved him!" (John 11:36).

Our view of Jesus will directly impact how we counsel and convey him to those around us. Do we counsel like the Wonderful Counselor? Do friends and counselees experience us as able to sorrow with them, as acquainted with grief—ours and theirs—as sympathetic and empathetic, as deeply moved and troubled on their behalf, as loving them deeply?

LET'S COUNSEL LIKE THE HOLY SPIRIT, OUR DIVINE COMFORTER

The disciples' hearts were troubled when they learned that Jesus would be leaving (John 14:1–6). Because they were feeling abandoned, Jesus promised them, "I will not leave you as orphans" (John 14:18).

But how could Jesus leave them *and* not leave them? By sending them another Counselor, another Comforter, another Advocate, another Helper.

And I will ask the Father, and he will give you another Helper, to be with you forever, even the Spirit of truth, whom the world cannot receive, because it neither sees him nor knows him. You know him, for he dwells with you and will be in you. I will not leave you as orphans; I will come to you. . . . These things I have spoken to you while I am still with you. But the Helper, the Holy Spirit, whom the Father will send in my name, he will teach you all things and bring to your remembrance all that I have said to you. Peace I leave with you; my peace I give to you. Not as the world gives do I give to you. Let not your hearts be troubled, neither let them be afraid. (John 14:16–18, 25–27)

The Greek word for "Helper" is the noun form of the word we've been exploring in chapters 4 and 5: *parakaleo*. The Holy Spirit is our Divine *Parakaletic* Counselor living within us. He is our Encouragement Counselor. He is our Comforting Counselor.

We saw in chapter 2 that the Spirit practices his *parakaletic* counseling, in part, by grieving and groaning with us: "Likewise the Spirit helps us in our weakness. For we do not know what to pray for as we ought, but the Spirit himself intercedes for us with groanings too deep for words" (Romans 8:26). The Spirit identifies with us in our weaknesses, advocates for us in our struggles, and groans with us in our suffering.

Do we counsel like our Divine Comforter? Would our friends and counselees describe us as consoling, comforting, and encouraging? Would they experience us as identifying with them, advocating for them, and groaning with them?

LET'S CONSIDER OUR CALLING TO COUNSEL LIKE THE TRINITY

In the immediate context of God the Father as our Comforter, Paul commands us to comfort one another.

Blessed be the God and Father of our Lord Jesus Christ, the Father of mercies and God of all comfort, who comforts us in all our affliction, *so that we may be able to comfort those who are in any affliction, with the comfort with which we ourselves are comforted by God.* For as we share abundantly in Christ's sufferings, *so through Christ we share abundantly in comfort too.* If we are afflicted, it is for your comfort and salvation; and if we are comforted, it is for your comfort, which you experience when you patiently endure the same sufferings that we suffer. Our hope for you is unshaken, for we know that *as you share in our sufferings, you will also share in our comfort.* (2 Corinthians 1:3–7, emphases added)

Biblical counselors *are to be* biblical comforters because God is the Father of all comfort.

Biblical counselors *can be* biblical comforters if and when we turn to the God of all comfort for our own comfort when we face sorrows and trials. The best comfort givers are comfort receivers— those who have tasted the compassionate care of God for their own troubles. As God's infinite comfort flows into us, it then is to overflow out of us into our brothers and sisters.

This is why God calls the body of Christ to care for and suffer with one another: "But God has so composed the body, giving greater honor to the part that lacked it, that there may be no division in the body, but that the members may have the same care for one another. If one member suffers, all suffer together; if one member is honored, all rejoice together" (1 Corinthians 12:24–26). And it's why as individual members of the body of Christ, we are commanded to mourn with those who mourn, weeping with those who weep (Romans 12:15).

And this is why Paul follows the model of the Trinity and models for us Trinitarian counseling: "But we were gentle among you, like a nursing mother taking care of her own children. So, being affectionately desirous of you, we were ready to share with you not only the gospel of God but also our own selves, because you had become very dear to us" (1 Thessalonians 2:7–8).

ASSESSING OUR BIBLICAL COUNSELING

1. Do we counsel like God the Father? Do we sympathetically lament with others? Do others experience us as their caring advocate, as their concerned protector, as their empathetic ally?

2. Do we counsel like God the Son? Do we sorrow with others? Do we grieve with others? Are we sympathetic toward and empathetic with others? Are we deeply moved by the suffering of others?

3. Do we counsel like God the Spirit? Are we consoling, comforting, and encouraging? Do we identify and groan with others?

4. Do we counsel like the Trinity? Does the comfort of the Father, Son, and Holy Spirit overflow from the Trinity to us and then spill over to our brothers and sisters?

MISTAKE #6:

WE VIEW PEOPLE ONE-DIMENSIONALLY
INSTEAD OF COMPREHENSIVELY

AS I supervise counselors, I've notice that we counselors often have our "pet" perspective of people. We each tend to view others through a primary lens. In biblical counseling:

- Some of us see people primarily through the lens of *lovers and relators*, so we try to spot sinful idols of the heart and seek to encourage a return to our first love for Christ and sacrificial love for others.
- Others of us might view people mainly as *thinkers and meaning-makers*, and thus our counseling focuses on exposing wrong thinking and renewing the mind.
- Still others perhaps look at people predominantly as *doers and choosers*, and our counseling seeks to help people to put off old behaviors and the motivations associated with them and put on new behaviors and motivations.
- Some may see people primarily as *feelers*, and our major approach is to identify with people's emotions, help them lament to God, and equip them to grow in emotional maturity.

While each of these perspectives has something to offer, in isolation none is comprehensive or balanced. And although few of us see people *only* through one lens, many of us magnify one lens out of proportion. Perhaps this one-dimensional focus is our way of trying to manage complexity.

I remember biblical counseling pioneer David Powlison sharing at a Biblical Counseling Coalition Leadership Summit how it saddened him that his article on idols of the heart had taken on a life of its own.[1] He wrote it to enrich our biblical counseling mindset about people's struggles. Instead, some biblical counselors began to see people *only* through this *one* lens of heart idolatry.

BIBLICAL COUNSELING MUST BE COMPREHENSIVE IN UNDERSTANDING

In 2010, I had the privilege of facilitating the process of more than three dozen international biblical counseling leaders collaborating for nearly a year to develop the "Confessional Statement" of the Biblical Counseling Coalition. One of the twelve statements focuses on the truth that the Bible's understanding of people is rich and robust, complex and comprehensive. Consider the wording:

> We believe that biblical counseling should focus on the full range of human nature created in the image of God (Genesis 1:26–28). A comprehensive biblical understanding sees human beings as *relational (spiritual and social), rational, volitional, emotional, and physical*. Wise counseling takes the whole person seriously in his or her whole life context. It helps people to embrace all of life face-to-face with Christ so they become more like Christ in their *relationships, thoughts, motivations, behaviors, and emotions*.

> We recognize the complexity of the relationship between the *body and soul* (Genesis 2:7). Because of this, we seek to remain sensitive to physical factors and organic issues that affect people's lives. In our desire to help people comprehensively, we seek to apply God's Word to people's lives amid bodily strengths and weaknesses. We encourage a thorough assessment and sound treatment for any suspected physical problems.

We recognize the complexity of the connection between *people and their social environment.* Thus we seek to remain sensitive to the impact of *suffering* and of the great variety of significant *social-cultural factors* (1 Peter 3:8–22). In our desire to help people comprehensively, we seek to apply God's Word to people's lives amid both *positive and negative social experiences.* We encourage people to seek appropriate practical aid when their problems have a component that involves education, work life, finances, legal matters, criminality (either as a victim or a perpetrator), and other social matters.[2]

God calls all biblical counselors toward this type of comprehensive understanding of people—an understanding developed throughout the Scriptures.

BIBLICAL COUNSELORS NEED TO UNDERSTAND PEOPLE— BIBLICALLY

A chapter this size could never adequately capture the Bible's robust understanding of people. (For a lengthier discussion of a biblical understanding of people, see chapters 6 and 7 of *Gospel-Centered Counseling*).[3] My more limited purpose here is twofold: (1) to briefly outline a scriptural understanding of people, and (2) to succinctly summarize some of the biblical counseling implications of a comprehensive understanding of people.

As bearers of God's image, we are multidimensional, as illustrated in figure 1 (below). This knowledge helps us to carefully consider the many factors at play in a person's heart and life when we seek to provide meaningful, biblical care. As you view the center of the larger concentric circles, you'll see an arrow directing you to three smaller concentric circles. These three areas of self-aware being, social being, and spiritual being are each aspects of who we are as relational beings. Compassionate and comprehensive care views each of these aspects as worthy of our attention and involvement.

FIGURE 1: A BIBLICAL UNDERSTANDING OF PEOPLE—OUR SOUL AND OUR SITUATION

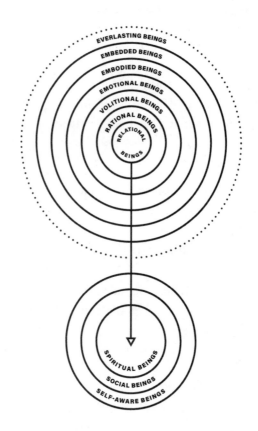

1. We Are *Everlasting* Beings: Ecclesiastes 3:11; Luke 4:1–13; Acts 17:28; 1 Corinthians 10:31

God designed us for relationship with him as our ultimate environment. We are *coram Deo* (face-to-face-with-God) beings. Whatever other painful or positive situations we experience, God is our ultimate context. Notice the dotted line around this first category—it communicates that God is our circumference and our reference point. The other aspects of our human experience and human nature are all incorporated in this ultimate God-reality. Thus, while we never minimize the external event or internal experiences of our counselees, we always seek to help our counselees see those experiences within the broader context of God's affectionate sovereignty—his infinite love and power.

2. We Are *Embedded* Beings (Life Situation): Matthew 26:40; 1 Corinthians 12:24–27

We are a "situated soul"—God embedded us in a world in which he designed us to be connected to and impacted by one another and by our life situation. It was not good for Adam to be socially alone even while in a perfect spiritual relationship with God in the perfect Garden. Thus, it is hyper-spiritual and anti-scriptural to assume that closeness to God totally shields us from the impact of life in a fallen world. As biblical counselors, we take into account the past and present life situation of our counselees. We recognize and address the vital importance and influence of human relationships and the joy and pain derived from those human relationships. We seek to understand the impact on our counselees of the painful past and present situations they experience (suffering, sickness, trauma, etc.).

3. We Are *Embodied* Physical Beings: Genesis 2:7; Matthew 26:41; 2 Corinthians 4:7

God designed us as a complex combination of body and soul. The state and condition of our outer person impacts our inner person and vice versa. Thus, while understanding the vital importance of the soul, biblical counselors do not neglect our bodily realities and their connection to our inner condition (see chapter 8 for a fuller development of the importance of our body-soul connection).

4. We Are *Emotional* Beings: Psalm 139:13–14; Matthew 27:46

God designed us to experience life richly and to feel deeply. Emotions are God's idea. The Word encourages us to address our feelings face-to-face with our Father. Thus, biblical counselors embrace the legitimate place of emotions and our emotionality and seek to engage people as emotional beings and help them to face their emotions candidly and bring their emotions honestly to God (see chapter 7 for a fuller development of the importance of emotions in biblical counseling).

5. We Are *Volitional* Beings: Joshua 24:15; Matthew 26:39

God designed us to choose courageously. We have a will and motivational core that purposefully pursues either a Godward or a non-Godward direction in life. Thus, biblical counselors help people to assess the heart motivations behind their behaviors and align those motivations and behaviors with the ultimate motivations of loving God (worship) and loving people (ministry).

6. We Are *Rational* Beings: Matthew 6:9; Romans 8:31–39; 12:1–2; Philippians 2:5–11

God designed us to think wisely, or, as the Reformers said, God designed us to think God's thoughts after him. We have the capacity to perceive life either through Christ-centered lenses or through world-focused lenses. Thus, biblical counselors enlighten counselees to evaluate their circumstances through the lens of the cross of Christ, rather than evaluating Christ through the lens of their circumstances.

7. We Are *Relational* Beings: Matthew 22:35–40; John 4:1–26

God designed us to love sacrificially. He designed us with a three-fold relationality: to ourselves, to others, and to himself.

a. We Are *Self-Aware* Relational Beings: Psalm 42:5; Luke 2:49; John 17:20–26; Romans 12:3

God designed us, not like animals to live on instinct nor like computers to live on programing, but as image bearers with a sense of self-awareness. Ultimately, God designed us so that our identity is embedded in who and whose we are in Christ. This is why Paul exhorts us in Romans 12:3 to think of ourselves in view of our faith relationship to Christ. Thus, biblical counselors help counselees to live according to their new identity in Christ.

b. We Are *Social* Relational Beings: Genesis 2:18; Matthew 22:39–40; John 10:11

Earlier we noted that we are *embedded* beings—this highlights the importance of recognizing the impact we have on one another and the influence of those human relationships. Now with this category of *social relational* beings, we are highlighting that God designed us for relationships with one another of *mutual sacrificial ministry*. Thus, biblical counselors help counselees to put off self-centered relationships with others and to put on other-centered relationships with people—in the strength and through the love of Christ.

c. We Are *Spiritual* Relational Beings: Matthew 22:35–38; Luke 23:46

We are worshipping beings. God designed us to exalt him, enjoy him, and entrust our souls to him. The holy of holies of our soul is our capacity to relate to the Trinity. Figure 1 seeks to capture this concept by picturing *spiritual relational* beings as the center or core of who we are. Thus, the difference between biblical counseling and secular counseling is that we embed every aspect of human experience and human nature within our relationship to God. For example, when we engage people about the impact of their past family relationships, we are always pondering together, "How are you fitting God into these past painful relationships?" When we enter people's emotional trauma, we are always pondering together, "Where and who was God for you when you experienced this? What would it mean for you to entrust your soul to the Father and to soothe your soul in your Savior as you are feeling all of this?"

BIBLICAL COUNSELING IMPLICATIONS: *THE CHRISTLIKE MATURITY INVENTORY*

So what? What difference does a comprehensive biblical understanding of people (figure 1) make for biblical counseling and daily Christian living?

The ultimate goal of biblical counseling is Christlikeness that glorifies God. Yet we often use the phrase *growing in Christlikeness* in the abstract, without a clear, biblical picture of what Christ was

like. The Christlike Maturity Inventory (CMI) provides us with a
real-life understanding of what it means to be like Christ.

Biblical counselors can use the CMI in two primary ways. First,
it provides the counselor with a set of goals for counseling that we
can use to assure that our counseling is comprehensively focused.
It is a grid to help us ask assessment questions like, Am I focusing only or primarily with this counselee as an emotional being?
Or, am I focusing holistically with this person—over time in our
counseling—on each aspect of his or her soul and life experiences?

Second, we can use the CMI with counselees as a homework
assignment or growth assessment. By discussing each category, we
expand our counselees' understanding of what Christlikeness looks
like, and we help them begin to be their own best biblical counselor as they evaluate their growth and develop a comprehensive
biblical growth plan.

1. Our Christlike Maturity Inventory with *Everlasting* Beings: Designed for God as Our Ultimate Environment— Luke 4:1–13; Acts 17:28; 1 Corinthians 10:31

Our CMI Question: Like Christ, do our counselees judge
their circumstances through the grid of their Father's love, rather
than judging their Father's love by their circumstances?

In Luke 4:1–13, rather than being in a perfect garden, Jesus
is in a desolate wilderness. Yet he goes there "full of the Spirit"
and "led by the Spirit." As biblical counselors, we seek to help our
counselees face their empty circumstances filled with the presence
and power of God.

2. Our Christlike Maturity Inventory with *Embedded* Beings (Life Situation): Designed to Be Connected to and Impacted by One Another—Matthew 26:40; 1 Corinthians 12:24–27

Our CMI Counselor Question: Like Christ, do our counselees
candidly experience life in this broken world? Our CMI Counselee
Questions: To what degree do I honestly face the pain of life in a fallen
world? How could I follow Christ's model of candidly facing loss?

In Matthew 26:40, our perfect Savior, in a perfect relationship with his Father, experienced the disappointment of human relationships. Rather than an over-spiritualized response, Jesus honestly responded and candidly expressed his sorrow and disappointment. "And he came to the disciples and found them sleeping. And he said to Peter, 'So, could you not watch with me one hour?'" (Matthew 26:40). As biblical counselors, we take into account the impact of fallen human relationships, and we encourage our counselees to face those situations like Christ—candidly.

3. Our Christlike Maturity Inventory with *Embodied* Beings: Designed to Be Body-Soul Beings—Genesis 2:7; Matthew 11:28–30; 26:41; 2 Corinthians 4:7

Our CMI Counselor Question: Like Christ, do our counselees depend second by second on the Spirit because they know they have the treasure of the image of God in jars of clay (2 Corinthians 4:7)? Our CMI Counselee Question: To what degree do I allow my physical weaknesses and limitations to motivate me to cling dependently to God's infinite strength?

In Matthew 26:41, Jesus expressed the frailty of the human body: "the spirit indeed is willing, but the flesh is weak." Throughout his life and ministry, Jesus the God-man rested his physical body and replenished his physical and spiritual strength in the Father through the Spirit. As biblical counselors, we recognize the weakness of the human body and its impact on the human soul, and we help counselees come to Christ for rest of their weary bodies and souls (Matthew 11:28–30).

4. Our Christlike Maturity Inventory with *Emotional* Beings: Designed to Feel Deeply—Psalm 139:13–14; Matthew 27:46

Our CMI Counselor Question: Like Christ, do our counselees address their feelings face-to-face with their heavenly Father? Our CMI Counselee Question: To what degree do I soothe my soul in my Savior by openly lamenting to Christ all that I feel?

What does Christlike emotionality look like? Is it a stoic refusal to face and express what we feel? Not according to Jesus's example. Hanging on the cross, "Jesus cried out with a loud voice, saying, 'Eli, Eli, lema sabachthani?' that is, 'My God, my God, why have you forsaken me?'" (Matthew 27:46). Jesus didn't deny his experience or his feelings. He didn't just vent his feelings. Jesus lamented his feelings to his Father. As biblical counselors, we encourage our counselees to openly lament their situation and their souls to their sympathetic Savior.

5. Our Christlike Maturity Inventory with *Volitional* Beings: Designed to Choose Courageously—Joshua 24:15; Matthew 26:39

Our CMI Counselor Question: Like Christ, do our counselees surrender and entrust their will to their heavenly Father's will? Our CMI Counselee Question: To what degree do I surrender my will to my Father's will?

In Matthew 26:39, Jesus fell on his face and prayed, "My Father, if it be possible, let this cup pass from me; nevertheless, not as I will, but as you will." As biblical counselors, we assist our counselees to become more like Christ, who faced his choices honestly, chose courageously, and related submissively to his Father.

6. Our Christlike Maturity Inventory with *Rational* Beings: Designed to Think Wisely—Matthew 6:9; Romans 8:31–39; 12:1–2; Philippians 2:5–11

Our CMI Counselor Questions: Like Christ, do our counselees interpret life through the grid of the Father's holy love displayed on the cross of Christ? Like Christ, do our counselees have a mindset of living to glorify the Father by sacrificially loving others? Our CMI Counselee Questions: To what degree do I interpret life through the lens of the cross? To what degree do I evidence the mind of Christ by living to glorify God and minister to others?

Philippians 2:5 calls us to take on the mind of Christ. Philippians 2:6–11 then describes the focus of Christ's mindset— what will glorify God and what will minister to others? Philippians 2:1–4 (like Romans 12:1–2) explains that mind renewal always starts with a renewed awareness of the mercy, grace, and love of God. As biblical counselors, we enlighten our counselees to who God is as *the* foundation for renewing their minds.

7. Our Christlike Maturity Inventory with *Self-Aware* Relational Beings: Designed for Relationship with Ourself (Identity in Christ)—Psalm 42:5; Luke 2:49; John 17:20–26; Romans 12:3

Our CMI Counselor Question: Like Christ, do our counselees find their identity in their relationship to their Father? Our CMI Counselee Question: To what degree do I understand and apply my biblical identity in Christ?

While our human relationships surely shape our sense of self, ultimately our relationship to God must be the final source for our identity. This is how twelve-year-old Jesus lived. Jesus shared with his parents, "Why were you looking for me? Did you not know that I must be in my Father's house?" (Luke 2:49). This is how thirty-three-year-old Jesus lived: "Father, I desire that they also, whom you have given me, may be with me where I am, to see my glory that you have given me because you loved me before the foundation of the world" (John 17:24). As biblical counselors, we help our counselees to source their identity in Christ.

8. Our Christlike Maturity Inventory with *Social* Relational Beings: Designed for Sacrificial Relationships with One Another—Genesis 2:18; Matthew 20:28; 22:39–40; John 10:11; 15:13

Our CMI Counselor Question: Like Christ, do our counselees make sacrificial loving ministry the goal of their relationships to others? Our CMI Counselee Question: To what degree do I evidence Christlike sacrificial love for others?

Jesus came not to be served but to serve (Matthew 20:28). He is the good shepherd who lays down his life for his sheep (John 10:11). Biblical counselors seek to help counselees pursue the goal of ultimate love—laying down our lives for others (John 15:13).

9. Our Christlike Maturity Inventory with *Spiritual Relational Beings*: Designed for Worshipful Relationship with God—Matthew 22:35–40; Luke 23:46

Our CMI Counselor Question: Like Christ, do our counselees entrust their souls to their Father's good heart? Our CMI Counselee Question: To what degree does the chief end of my life focus on exalting God, entrusting myself to God, and enjoying God?

Worship is exalting God's good heart, entrusting ourselves to his good heart, and intimately enjoying his good heart. Jesus, hanging on the cross, moments away from dying for us as he takes upon his soul all our sin, entrusts his soul to his Father's good heart: "Father, into your hands I commit my spirit!" (Luke 23:46). As biblical counselors, this is the ultimate goal of our counseling—helping our counselees, with whatever trauma, trouble, and turmoil they are facing, to believe that God is good even when life is bad, and then to entrust their souls to their good, good Father.

What are the goals and the focus of your counseling? When we view people one-dimensionally, then our goals become shallow and out-of-balance. But when we view people biblically, then our goals are rich and comprehensive.

ASSESSING OUR BIBLICAL COUNSELING

1. As biblical counselors, do we have a "pet" perspective of people—viewing them through one primary lens instead of viewing them comprehensively?
2. Do we believe that biblical counseling should focus on the full range of human nature created in the image of God (Genesis 1:26–28), comprehensively understanding counselees as *relational (spiritual, social, and self-aware), rational, volitional, emotional, and physical* beings?
3. As biblical counselors, are *we* growing in Christlike maturity as evidenced by the nine biblical categories in the CMI?
4. As biblical counselors, do we seek to help our counselees to grow in Christlike maturity as evidenced by the nine biblical categories in the CMI?

MISTAKE #7:

WE DEVALUE EMOTIONS INSTEAD OF
SEEING EMOTIONS AS GOD'S IDEA

WHEN IT comes to emotions, we seem disposed to extremes, even in the Christian world. Some of us act as if emotions are a result of the fall, so we stuff them or ignore them. Others of us act as if emotions are king, and we allow them to rule us.

Some of us as biblical counselors seem to view emotions as not worthy of being considered part of the image of God. We accept that God created us with a soul to *relate*, a mind to *think*, and a will to *choose*. But we act as if emotions were *not* God's idea. We see emotions more as a cursing than a blessing: more harm than good; suppress them; ignore them; don't have them.

Some not only devalue emotions; they demean them. We'll often hear, "Don't trust your emotions." This is shared as a blanket statement implying that somehow emotions are "more fallen" than our desires, beliefs, and motivations. It would be more biblically accurate to say, "Don't trust any desires, beliefs, motivations, or emotions that are not being surrendered to the Spirit's control and evaluated through the grid of God's Word."

GOD'S ORIGINAL DESIGN FOR OUR EMOTIONS

What does the Bible teach about our emotions? What model of Christlike emotionality do we find in God's Word? If we are to live godly lives—Christlike lives—then we need God's perspective on emotions. And if we are to counsel biblically, then we need a biblical, practical theology of emotions. (For a fuller examination of the Bible's teaching on emotions, see *What Does the Bible Teach About Our Emotions? Learning the ABCs of Emotional Intelligence.*[1])

We've forgotten that when God paused to ponder his image bearers, he declared that they—emotions included—were "very good" (Genesis 1:31). Feelings were God's idea.

God created us in his image, including his emotional image. As John Piper notes, "God's emotional life is infinitely complex beyond our ability to fully comprehend."[2] Our emotionality is designed by God and like God. Our emotions were created *very good.*

EMOTIONS: FEARFULLY AND WONDERFULLY MADE
Emotions are God-given. Adam had them before the fall. Christ has them. Emotions are not sinful; they are beneficial and, yes, even beautiful.

The psalmist understood this. In Psalm 139—the classic passage describing God's utmost care in creating us—*emotionality is the one aspect of our inner personality* specifically referenced: "For you created my *inmost being*; you knit me together in my mother's womb" (Psalm 139:13 NIV, emphasis added). "Inmost being" is kidneys or reins in the KJV. Psalm 73:21 uses the same word to mean grieved and embittered. And in Proverbs 23:16, the kidneys are the place of rejoicing and gladness.

Hebrew language expert Hans Wolff explains that the Semitic language uses terms for kidneys, reins, stomach, bowels, and womb to describe the feeling states.[3] As we literally experience and feel an emotion in our physical being, we feel an emotion in our inner being. That's why we say things like, I have butterflies in my stomach.

God created your inmost being, your kidneys, your emotions. Your *emotions* are fearfully and wonderfully made—by God. In fact, your emotions are *the one element* that God highlights as having been fearfully and wonderfully made.

WHY DO WE FEEL WHAT WE FEEL?

Why did our heavenly Father create us with emotions? What is their purpose and function? The root of the word *emotion* is *motere*, from the Latin verb "to move," plus the prefix "e" meaning "to move away." This suggests that a tendency to act is implicit in every emotion. All emotions are, in essence, inclinations to act and react. This means that *God designed our emotions to put us in motion.*

Emotions represent an inner response that motivates outward action—emotions signal the mind to go into high gear. To understand this biblically, consider 1 Peter 5:7–8 (NIV): "Cast all your anxiety on him because he cares for you. Be alert and of sober mind. Your enemy the devil prowls around like a roaring lion looking for someone to devour."

We often fail to relate these two verses even though they appear together in Scripture. Anxiety, like all emotions, is an emotion that motivates us to act. Our emotions and our mind sense something that we perceive to be dangerous—a threat.

We can respond to that anxiety-provoking situation with fear of people and unnecessary self-protection—with fallen emotional responses. Or we can respond to that anxiety-provoking situation by casting our anxiety on him *and* by being alert and vigilant. We could describe the creation (pre-fall) side of anxiety as *vigilance*—the ability to pick up on cues in our world and to respond in a God-dependent, other-protecting way.

We don't need to think of emotions, including anxiety, as always sinful. We could take what Paul said in Ephesians 4 about anger and paraphrase it to include 1 Peter 5:7–8 with anxiety.

> Be anxious, but do not sin. Instead, when your emotional sensors detect a threat, then cast your anxiety upon the Lord. Use your anxiety to warn yourself to keep alert and vigilant. Don't be like Adam in the garden who went off sentry duty when the serpent tempted him and Eve.

Instead, be like Christ who was always on sentry duty to protect his disciples against the attacks of the Evil One.

Instead of seeing emotions as only evil or fallen, we need to understand that God designed emotions to play a crucial role that moves us to do a double-check, to look *outward and inward*. Emotions are our "inner sentinel" that connect us to our inner and outer world.

Now we can suggest working definitions of emotions:

- Emotions are our God-given capacity to connect our inner and outer world by experiencing our world and responding to those experiences.
- Our emotional capacity includes the ability to internally experience and respond to a full-range of both *positive* (pleasant) and *negative* (painful) inner feelings.

A BIBLICAL MODEL FOR UNDERSTANDING OUR COMPLEX EMOTIONAL RESPONSES

To understand our emotions, recall from the previous chapter how God designed our inner person. We've said that God designed us as emotional beings. However, that does not mean that we are only or primarily emotional beings. Nor does it mean that our emotions are meant to control us. Instead, God designed us so that our emotions submit to and respond to our beliefs and convictions. Though no linear outline can encompass the rich inner workings of our inner life, we can begin to picture the interaction of emotions, beliefs, desires, and motivation like this:

1. What we believe (Rational Direction; Romans 12:1–2)
2. about God and life (Relational Affection; Psalm 42:1–2)
3. informs the direction we choose to pursue (Volitional Motivation; Joshua 24:15), and
4. impacts our experiential/emotional response (Emotional Reaction; Ephesians 4:17–19) to our world.

- What we believe→about God and life→informs the direction we choose to pursue→and impacts our experiential/emotional response to our world.

Let's consider again how this plays out in 1 Peter 5:7–8. The context of this passage is a Christian response to suffering and persecution. Notice the key to how we respond to suffering—it's in the phrase "because he cares for you." We cast our anxiety on him *as a response* to our conviction that he cares for us.

- Our belief about God (that he cares for us) is what motivates our godly response (casting our cares on God and vigilantly resisting the devil) to feelings of anxiety.
- Godly beliefs (rational direction) encourage and incite godly affections (spiritual affections), which in turn prompt godly motivation and actions (volitional motivation) and ultimately encourage Christlike handling of our emotions (emotional reactions).

GOD DESIGNED OUR EMOTIONS TO INTERACT WITH OUR INNER AND OUTER WORLD

Now let's take this introductory theology of our inner life and consider a practical biblical model for understanding emotions. As we do this, realize that we are taking the intensity and complexity of emotions and placing them in "outline form." We all know that we can't bullet point our feelings. We all understand that our feelings are complicated, messy, real, and raw. Yet it is helpful to counselors and counselees to bring some logical understanding to what can feel like the "illogic" of emotions.

- *Our External Situation + Our Internal Perceptions Provide the Inner and Outer Context for Our Emotional Response.*

We might summarize our complex emotional responses to *negative* situations like this:

- Negative Situation + Biblical Belief = Legitimate Painful Emotion (Sorrow, Sadness, etc.)
- Negative Situation + Unbiblical Belief = Illegitimate Painful Emotion (Hatred, Despair, etc.)

Your boss says to you, "You blew it." Your emotions react to this negative external situation *and* to your internal beliefs. What if you had a biblical belief: "I enjoy my boss's approval, but I don't *need* it, and I know that in Christ I am accepted by God"? Then you could likely respond with legitimate painful emotions such as sorrow, disappointment, or remorse (if you were in the wrong).

On the other hand, what if "fear of people" is a besetting sin in your heart? What if you believe you must have your boss's approval? Then you might respond with illegitimate negative emotions such as uncontrolled anger, depression to the point of despair, hopelessness, or hatred.

We might summarize our complex emotional responses to *positive* situations like this:

- Positive Situation + Biblical Belief = Legitimate Positive Emotion (Joy, Peace)
- Positive Situation + Unbiblical Belief = Illegitimate Positive Emotion (Pride, Self-Sufficiency, etc.)

Now let's say your boss says to you, "You always do A+ work!" You could respond to that positive external situation with a biblical belief like the following: I live for an audience of One—Christ, and I am glad that my Christlike work ethic glorifies my heavenly Father. You might then experience positive legitimate emotions like peace, joy, and contentment.

On the other hand, if your boss says, "You always do A+ work," and you are living for the praise of people, then you might experience illegitimate positive emotions like pride and arrogance.

In summary, *the key to our emotional reaction is our belief or perception about the meaning behind the event.* Events impact whether our emotions are *pleasant or painful.* Our longings, beliefs, and goals impact whether our emotional reaction is holy or sinful.

BIBLICAL COUNSELING AND OUR EMOTIONS

Of course, our emotional lives are never so nice and neat. The reality is that few of our external situations are only positive or negative, and few of our internal beliefs are only wise or foolish. Additionally, not only are emotions impacted by our beliefs; our beliefs are impacted by our emotions. Let's be honest—life is messy; emotions are messy!

This is the beautiful value of a biblical counseling relationship. With all the confusion of emotions, we need another person to help us sort out what is happening *to* us and what is happening *in* us.

However, biblical counselors can't be helpful unless we have a practical biblical theology of emotions. So the first need is for biblical counselors to realize that emotions are not to be devalued but are of great value. Emotions are not to be demeaned but are instead God-designed core aspects of the image of God in us. Biblical counselors value the God-designed role that emotions play in our Christian lives and relationships.

With this biblical insight, as biblical counselors we are freed to actively engage with and enter our counselees' emotional lives. This is the soul connection we emphasized in chapter 1. It's the empathetic interaction about suffering we highlighted in chapter 4. It's following the Trinity's model of compassionate commiseration described in chapter 5.

Then, as we enter our counselees' emotional world, we help them bring some rationality to their emotionality. We help them bring some theology to their subjective experience. We do this by engaging with our counselees about the Bible's teaching on emotions. As part of this process, I'll often give counselees the document mentioned earlier in this chapter, *What Does the Bible Teach About Our Emotions? Learning the ABCs of Emotional Intelligence.*[4] Now we do some raw trialoguing (see chapter 3). The nice, neat outlines of this chapter become messy and meaningful gospel conversations where we help our counselees relate God's truth and God himself to their emotional experiences.

ASSESSING OUR BIBLICAL COUNSELING

1. As biblical counselors, do we devalue and demean emotions, or do we see emotions as being of great value because they are God-designed aspects of the image of God?

2. How does it impact our biblical counseling when we realize that emotions were God's idea and that God specifically declares that our emotions are fearfully and wonderfully made?

3. In our biblical counseling, how well or how poorly are we using a biblical theology of our inner life? What we believe→about God and life→informs the direction we choose to pursue→and impacts our experiential/emotional response to our world.

4. In our biblical counseling, how well or how poorly are we using a practical theology of understanding our emotions as we engage with and enlighten our counselees?

MISTAKE #8:

WE MINIMIZE THE COMPLEXITY OF THE BODY-SOUL INTERCONNECTION

THIS CHAPTER, along with the previous two, form a mini-trilogy within this larger ten-chapter work. In chapter 6, we addressed our need to develop and follow a comprehensive biblical understanding of people. In chapter 7, we explored how at times we devalue the role of our emotional nature. Now we'll consider how biblical counselors sometimes minimize the nature of our complex body-soul connection.

Because we are soul physicians and soul caregivers, we naturally focus on matters of the heart. Most of us as biblical counselors are not trained in the medical field, so we wisely avoid offering medical guidance. Yet, our appropriate emphasis on the soul can morph into a *sole focus on the soul*. While supervising biblical counselors, I've seen this show itself in several of the following ways.

- We sometimes fail to consider the impact of physical factors and physiological issues.
- At times we neglect the need for a complete physical checkup.
- We do not take seriously issues like diet, exercise, rest, and sleep.
- We fail to apply biblical teaching on the interrelationship of the body and soul.
- We are at times uninformed on the potential impact of trauma (physical and emotional) on the brain. As some

say, "the body keeps the score." Or as I say, "the physical brain sometimes seems to have a mind of its own."

• We sometimes demean the use of psychotropic medications even for the most severe issues such as schizophrenia, bipolar depression, or major depression.

To avoid these and other errors, we need a Creation-Fall-Redemption understanding of our body-soul connection. Understanding the way our physiology affects our emotional and mental constitution is another key to perceiving the many facets of an individual's situation and struggles.

CREATION: DESIGNED BY GOD, WE EXIST AS A COMPLEX BODY-SOUL UNITY

In chapter 6, we examined the Biblical Counseling Coalition's statement on the body-soul connection. We repeat the most pertinent portion here:

> We recognize the complexity of the relationship between the body and soul (Genesis 2:7). Because of this, we seek to remain sensitive to physical factors and organic issues that affect people's lives. In our desire to help people comprehensively, we seek to apply God's Word to people's lives amid bodily strengths and weaknesses. We encourage a thorough assessment and sound treatment for any suspected physical problems.[1]

From the beginning, God created us as a complex, unified combination of dust and divinity, brain and mind, body and soul, flesh and spirit. "Then the LORD God formed the man of dust from the ground and breathed into his nostrils the breath of life, and the man became a living creature" (Genesis 2:7).

In biblical thinking, we do not have a body; we are embodied souls. The flesh is our whole life organized in corporal form— embodied personalities. Body (*bāśār* in Hebrew and *sarx* in Greek) represents humanity in a certain type of relationship to God—one of finitude, contingency, neediness, dependence, weakness, frailty, and mortality. God is infinite; we are finite.[2]

Our embodied souls are works of art fashioned by God, who fearfully and wonderfully handcrafted us (Psalm 139:13–16). We are God's handiwork: made, shaped, molded, clothed with skin and flesh, and knit together with bones and sinews (Job 10:3–12). We are not to despise our physicality[3] nor the fact that physical considerations may indeed play a role in a counselee's presenting struggle.

God has intricately interwoven the material and immaterial aspects of our beings as psychosomatic wholes. The life of Elijah in 1 Kings 18–19 illustrates the *impact of our body on our soul*. Elijah's traumatic external situation and his broken, tired, and weary body impacted his inner life. Part of God's solution for Elijah's spiritual depression was soul related—regaining a biblical perspective and a right connection to God. Part of God's solution was body related—rest, food, and sleep. And part of God's solution was situational—protection and removal from his unsafe environment. This multidimensional care from the Lord illustrates how we are to approach the hurting and weary counselee who comes to us for care.

Likewise, the Bible illustrates the *impact of our soul upon our body*. In Psalm 32, when David refused to confess his sins, his bones wasted away and his strength was sapped (vv. 3–4). The soul impacts the body; the body impacts the soul.

FALL: DEPRAVED BY SIN, WE ARE NOW A FALLEN EMBODIED SOUL

We are all a combination of body and soul, and since Genesis 3, both aspects of our person keenly feel the effects of the fall. We are fallen embodied souls living in a fallen world with a fallen physical brain in a fallen physical body.

Our bodies no longer function perfectly according to their original design. For example, our liver in our fallen body can become diseased. It can be impacted by the environment outside our body and by what we put into our body. Likewise, our physical brain in our fallen body can become diseased. It can be impacted by our external environment, such as social interactions and relational trauma. The brain can likewise be impacted by what we take into our body, as well as by genetic factors and the aging process.

We are not the way we were supposed to be. Sin has deeply impacted every aspect of our body-soul being.

REDEMPTION: RENEWED BY CHRIST, WE AWAIT OUR FINAL GLORIFICATION

The fall does not claim the final word. Redemption does. Paul explains that we have the treasure of the glory of God embedded in bodies that are jars of clay (2 Corinthians 4:7). A few verses later, Paul describes our outward life (our flesh, our body, our temporal existence) as fading away, yet our inward person (our soul, our spirit, our eternal existence) being renewed daily (we are progressing daily in inner growth in Christ).

Our body includes our brain, organs, neurons, cells, flesh, chemicals, glands, etc., all of which we can either offer to God as servants of righteousness or offer to sin as servants of unrighteousness. Our "flesh" can be the instrument of ingrained righteousness or ingrained evil (Romans 6:11–23; 16:18; Philippians 3:19–21). When we live as if the body is all we have and surrender our members to unrighteousness, then we are "fleshly." When we live as if this world is all there is and that our temporal time is all the time we have, then we are "worldly." When we use our bodies to live for God's glory, then we are "godly."[4]

In Romans 8, Paul reminds us that, like all creation, we groan for the day when our redeemed inner person will be glorified. And we "wait eagerly for adoption as sons, the redemption of our bodies" (Romans 8:23). We long for the resurrection of the dead. The body that is "sown is perishable; what is raised is imperishable. It is sown in dishonor; it is raised in glory. It is sown in weakness; it is raised in power. It is sown a natural body; it is raised a spiritual body. If there is a natural body, there is also a spiritual body" (1 Corinthians 15:42–44).

THE BRAIN/MIND AND PSYCHOTROPIC MEDICINE

Addressing the body-soul connection inevitably leads to the important issue of psychotropic medication. This discussion often prompts strong reactions among biblical counselors. Surely, the short section that follows will not settle the discussion—and will potentially unsettle some people. Some may be concerned that medication is not given enough credence, while others might contend that medication is given too much credit. If you desire more depth than this section can provide, I'd encourage you to read the works of Daniel Berger, Mike Emlet, Laura Hendrickson, Charles Hodges, Robert B. Somerville, and Ed Welch—writers who provide a diversity of biblical counseling perspectives.[5]

As we saw in chapter 6, it is naïve and potentially harmful to treat people as one-dimensional beings. First, this means that we must take into account possible physiological contributions to life struggles. Psychiatrist and biblical counselor Dr. Laura Hendrickson explained:

> It is dangerous to assume that all emotional struggles can be changed by strictly "spiritual means." For some, spirituality includes embracing physical weakness. When we ignore the importance of the body, we misunderstand what it means to trust God. It is wrong to place extra burdens on those who suffer emotionally by suggesting that all they need to do is surrender to God to make their struggles go away.[6]

Secondly, seeing a person comprehensively means that we should never view psychotropic interventions as the sole solution for life issues. Sadly, it is common in our culture today for specialists of many kinds to view people primarily from a material, physical lens, which leads to the use of psychotropic medication as a primary resource. When that happens, what could be one part of the curative process can be used instead as justification to ignore the soul issues that may be connected to various emotional and mental struggles.

These concerns are not limited to the biblical counseling world. Psychiatrists such as Allen Frances and Edward Shorter believe the right medication prescribed in the right dosage at the right time can at times be beneficial. However, they also believe we've convinced ourselves that a variety of merely human experiences—temporary bouts of sadness or excitement or distraction—are in fact pathologies that need to be treated with drugs.[7]

In addition to legitimate concern with a worldview that recognizes only the material world, it is also wise to acknowledge that psychotropic medication is still in its infancy. We would be naïve not to take into account their side effects and their low current success rate in actually helping troubled people.[8]

Hendrickson encouraged a nuanced, balanced perspective on the relationship between spiritual and physical approaches to our emotional and mental struggles. When used as part of a comprehensive, whole-person approach, she saw the potential use of psychotropic medication as an issue of Christian liberty (Romans 14–15) and biblical discernment (Philippians 1:9–11).

I believe we can agree that our bodies play an important role in our emotions without insisting that all painful feelings are due to a disease. I also don't think that it's a sin or an admission of weakness to take psychiatric drugs. But taking a medication without considering spiritual issues may leave the most important factor unaddressed. In fact, it's been my experience, through twenty years of psychiatric and biblical counseling practice, that a medicine-only approach doesn't resolve emotional pain completely or permanently in most cases.[9]

WHAT CHURCH HISTORY TEACHES ABOUT PHYSICIANS OF THE BODY AND THE SOUL

Sometimes when we initiate conversations about the role of the body in matters of the soul, some may suspect us of having surrendered to the modern psychiatric worldview. In light of these concerns, I find it helpful to study how our forerunners in the faith perceived these issues.

Though Martin Luther held a strong spiritual focus, he did not see every issue as a spiritual issue in terms of cause and cure. Luther worked hand in hand with physicians because he saw ministers as physicians of the soul and doctors as physicians of the body. For Luther, the wise physician of soul or body distinguishes causes and then prescribes the appropriate cures.

In one table talk, Luther states that though Satan was the first cause of sickness and death, this did not negate the need for physical remedies: "Generally speaking, therefore, I think that all dangerous diseases are blows of the devil. For this, however, he employs the instruments of nature."[10] Since this is the case, when one battles sickness, the battle is on two levels, both the spiritual and the physical. He further reflects, "God also employs means for the preservation of health, such as sleep for the body, food, and drink, for he does nothing except through instruments."[11] Therefore, it is appropriate and necessary to treat the whole person. He goes on to say,

> Accordingly a physician is our Lord God's mender of the body, as we theologians are his healers of the spirit; we are to restore what the devil has damaged. So a physician administers *theriaca* (an antidote for poison) when Satan gives poison. Healing comes from the application of nature to the creature . . . . It's our Lord God who created all things, and they are good. Where- fore it's permissible to use medicine, for it is a creature of God. Thus I replied to Hohndorf, who inquired of me when he heard from Karlstadt that it's not permissi- ble to make use of medicine. I said to him, "Do you eat when you're hungry?"[12]

On the other hand, when convinced that an issue was spiritual in nature, Luther did not hesitate to call for spiritual rather than medicinal cures. He writes to his friend John Agricola concerning John's wife: "Her illness is, as you see, rather of the mind than of the body. I am comforting her as much as I can, with my knowledge."[13]

Two concepts stand out in Luther's response. First, it was important for Luther that causes be discerned. Second, even when he sensed that causes were spiritual, Luther did not believe he was the lone expert with the final word on everything. The quoted passage and others reflect a pastor who, with prayerful, Spirit-led discernment, was willing to refer to physicians when the issue was physical, and refer to other Christians when the issue was spiritual but beyond his realm of expertise.

Luther continued by telling Agricola,

> In a word, her disease is not for the apothecaries (as they call them), nor is it to be treated with the salves of Hippocrates, but by constantly applying plasters of Scripture and the Word of God. For what has conscience to do with Hippocrates? Therefore, I would dissuade you from the use of medicine and advise the power of God's Word.[14]

Luther speaks to those today who maintain a materialistic worldview that assumes that every issue is biologically based and, therefore, treatable *only* by psychotropic medication. He also speaks to those today who maintain a spiritualistic worldview that assumes that every issue is *solely* soul-based and, therefore, treatable *only* by speaking the truth in love.

SO WHAT? BIBLICAL COUNSELING AND THE BODY-SOUL CONNECTION

Mike Emlet is a biblical counselor and a former physician. He captures well in modern language ideas that overlap with what Luther taught five hundred years ago. His summary provides wise and practical counsel for how we can apply the biblical teaching about the body-soul connection to our actual practice of biblical counseling.

> We are body-spirit creatures. We should not be surprised that a physical treatment such as medication may be associated with

symptomatic and perhaps more substantial change in people's lives.

Medication can be an appropriate and even necessary part of someone's care, depending on the specific nature of a person's struggle.

Yet, we must admit a great deal of remaining mystery about how psychoactive medications actually work in the human brain. We take care to remain balanced in our assessment of the efficacy of medications. We neither exalt them nor disregard them.

Even if we do view medication as a potential piece in a comprehensive ministry approach, we always seek to bring the riches of Christ's redemption to bear upon people's lives.

Sinners will always need mercy, grace, forgiveness, and supernatural power to love God and neighbor.

Sufferers will always need comfort, hope, and the will to persevere. Ultimately, these blessings are found not in a pill bottle . . . but in the person of Jesus Christ.[15]

ASSESSING OUR BIBLICAL COUNSELING

1. As soul physicians, does our emphasis on the soul morph into a sole focus on the soul that minimizes the complex interrelationship between the body and soul? Do we remain sensitive to physical factors and organic issues that affect people's lives? Do we encourage a thorough assessment and sound treatment for any suspected physical problems?

2. As soul physicians, do we understand and apply the Bible's Creation-Fall-Redemption teaching on the complex interrelationship of the body and soul—as designed by God, depraved by sin, and saved by grace?

3. As soul physicians, do we seek to understand the impact of the body on our counselee's soul? Do we seek to understand the soul's impact on our counselee's body?

4. Like Luther, as physicians of the soul, do we avoid a materialistic worldview that assumes every issue is exclusively
biologically based? And do we avoid a spiritualistic worldview that assumes every issue is exclusively soul-based?

MISTAKE #9:

WE MAXIMIZE SIN WHILE MINIMIZING GRACE

MOST OF us have a tendency to pull pendulums in one direction or the other. This was true of the Corinthians. In 1 Corinthians 5:1–5, Paul had to confront the Corinthians because they were *not* confronting the public sin of a member of the body of Christ. They were "winking at sin," minimizing sin, and refusing to use biblical discernment, judgment, and confrontation regarding sin.

Then the Corinthians responded to Paul's confrontation by confronting this brother. According to 2 Corinthians 2:5–11 (which many commentators believe reflects back on 1 Corinthians 5:1–5), the Corinthians got stuck in confronting him.

> Now if anyone has caused pain, he has caused it not to me, but in some measure—not to put it too severely—to all of you. For such a one, this punishment by the majority is enough, so you should rather turn to forgive and comfort him, or he may be overwhelmed by excessive sorrow. So I beg you to reaffirm your love for him. For this is why I wrote, that I might test you and know whether you are obedient in everything. Anyone whom you forgive, I also forgive. Indeed, what I have forgiven, if I have forgiven anything, has been for your sake in the presence of Christ, so that we would not be outwitted by Satan; for we are not ignorant of his designs. (2 Corinthians 2:5–11)

Paul says, "The confrontation worked! Your church discipline was sufficient. He confessed, repented, and is changing." Notice what Paul says next: "Instead, you ought to forgive and comfort him" (NIV). Instead, "reaffirm your love for him."

Why? So he will not be overwhelmed by excessive sorrow. Who is behind this excessive sorrow? The accuser of the brethren, Satan, who schemes to outwit us by heaping condemnation on us—sin without grace. If we maximize sin while minimizing grace, then we are actually joining Satan's condemning scheme. Of course, none of us would purposefully join Satan's scheme. By God's grace, all of us when we do confront sin are motivated by God's glory and our counselee's good/growth.

Consider the launch of the modern nouthetic counseling movement (circa 1970s). It defined nouthetic counseling as *confronting out of concern for change*. We confront because we're concerned for the counselee and concerned for the glory of God. We confront with the desire to encourage the counselee to put off the old ways and put on the new in-Christ ways.

In no way do we want to minimize the role of caring confronting (care-fronting) of sin. Instead, we seek to emphasize the danger of potentially maximizing sin while minimizing grace.

WHERE SIN ABOUNDS GRACE SUPERABOUNDS

Paul communicated the biblical emphasis on grace like this, "Where sin increased, grace abounded all the more" (Romans 5:20). I translate it like this: "Where sin abounds, grace superabounds!"

As biblical counselors, do we emphasize sin or grace? In our concern for confronting sin, do we sometimes inadvertently become sin-sniffers, idol-spotters, and sin-maximizers? Or as we confront sin, do we consciously communicate Christ's superabounding, amazing, infinite grace?

In church history, the Puritans modeled well this *both-and* focus on sin and grace. In dealing with an unrepentant, deceived, hardened sinner, Puritan soul physicians would seek to *load the conscience with guilt.* Though the phrase may sound harsh, it reflects the loving motivation of Hebrews 3:12–13 (NIV): "See to it, brothers and sisters, that none of you has a sinful, unbelieving heart that turns away from the living God. But encourage one another daily, as long as it is called 'Today,' so that none of you may be hardened by sin's deceitfulness."

The Puritans would never stop at sin but always magnified grace. With a repentant person and with persons with a tender conscience, Puritan soul physicians next sought to *lighten the conscience with grace.* They would help one another to grasp how wide, long, high, and deep is the love of Christ (Ephesians 3:18). They would encourage one another to see the Father through the lens of the parable of the prodigal son—a Father who runs to his repentant children, throws his arms around us, is filled with compassion for us, kisses us, calls us "son" or "daughter," celebrates with us, and insists that we put on the family attire because we've been reconciled by grace (Luke 15:20–24).

For the Puritans, we were not only sinners in the hands of an angry God. Even more, through Christ we are sons and daughters in the palms of our forgiving Father.

LET'S BE GRACE MAXIMIZERS, GRACE MAGNIFIERS, AND GRACE DISPENSERS

When I teach biblical reconciliation through care-fronting, I use a twin phrase to portray the relational reconciling process: *"It is horrible to sin, but it's wonderful to be forgiven!"*

Yes, of course biblical counselors must confront sin. However, if we only emphasized the horrors of sin, then we would be sin-maximizers who become sin-spotters. We would spot a sin, expose a sin, exhort the person toward change, and move on to the next counselee. But that's not comprehensive, compassionate reconciliation that also communicates "it's wonderful to be forgiven!" As ambassadors of reconciliation, biblical counselors are grace maximizers and grace dispensers.

Martin Luther understood our role as dispensers of grace. He reflected, "The word of a fellow-Christian has wonderful power. The voice of brethren and fellow Christians are to be heard and believed as the word and voice of God himself, as though God was speaking to them."[1] Biblical counselors share the Bible's truth about the Father's grace—we help one another to grasp grace.

Luther also understood how we should respond to a repentant brother.

> When we have laid bare our conscience to our brother and privately make known to him the evil that lurked within, we receive from our brother's lips the word of comfort spoken by God himself. And if we accept this in faith, we find peace in the mercy of God speaking to us through our brother.[2]

Biblical counselors speak words of comforting grace to our counselees—we lighten their conscience with grace. We probe passages and trialogue about how the God of grace and the grace of God make a difference in our counselee's soul.

According to Luther, we not only counsel others, we also provide ourselves with ongoing grace-focused self-counsel. When Satan schemed to overwhelm him with condemnation, Luther would confront Satan with grace.

> You say that the sins which we commit every day offend God, and therefore we are not saints. To this I reply: Mother love is stronger than the filth and scabbiness on a child, and so the love of God toward us is stronger than the dirt that clings to us. Accordingly, although we are sinners, we do not lose our filial relation on account of our filthiness, nor do we fall from grace on account of our sin.[3]

As biblical counselors, we equip our counselees to fish the grace-filled Scriptures, so they can defeat Satan's condemning lies with Christ's justifying and reconciling truth and grace.

Luther insisted that we hold up before our eyes the gospel mirror of grace in which we see our forgiving Father.

> For who is able to express what a thing it is, when a man is assured in his heart that God neither is nor will be angry with him, but will be forever a merciful and loving Father to him for Christ's sake? This is indeed a marvelous and incomprehensible liberty, to have the most high and sovereign Majesty so favorable to us. Wherefore, this is an inestimable liberty, that we are made free from the wrath of God forever.[4]

Luther models our motto as biblical counselors: *Where sin abounds; grace superabounds!*

We want to be Luther-like biblical counselors. Yes, we expose sin. But we also and even more expose grace. We help our counselees to identify Satan's works-oriented, law-based, condemnation-focused narratives that they are believing. We help our counselees to put off those lies and to put on—specific to their sin struggle—Christ's grace-oriented, forgiveness-based, justification narrative.

ASSESSING OUR BIBLICAL COUNSELING

1. Which do we emphasize as biblical counselors: sin or grace? In our concern for confronting sin, do we sometimes inadvertently become sin-sniffers, idol-spotters, and sin-maximizers? Or as we confront sin, do we consciously communicate Christ's superabounding, amazing, infinite grace?

2. As biblical counselors, are we like Paul in Romans 5:20, reminding one another that where sin abounds, grace superabounds?

3. As biblical counselors, are we like the Puritans—able to load the conscience with guilt *and* to lighten the conscience with grace? Like Luther, are we dispensers of Christ's gospel of grace?

4. As biblical counselors, are we loving ambassadors of reconciliation who seek to share that "it's horrible to sin, but it's wonderful to be forgiven"?

MISTAKE #10:

WE CONFUSE THE SUFFICIENCY OF SCRIPTURE WITH THE COMPETENCY OF THE COUNSELOR

THIS CHAPTER title—with words like *sufficiency* and *competency*—may seem like the most technical of these ten mistakes. However, this final topic may be one of the most practical.

I was recently contacted by a lay biblical counselor (let's call him Jim) who was just beginning his master of arts degree in biblical counseling. Jim was approached by a man who was hearing voices, among several other concerns. Jim explained:

> Bob, I've been excited to learn that the Scriptures are sufficient for all soul issues and that every Christian can become a competent biblical counselor. But the implication I feel like I'm hearing is that *since* the Scriptures are sufficient, *therefore* I should have the faith to take on *any* counseling issue that comes my way. I feel guilty for doubting whether I'm equipped to take on this case, but I'm a rookie counselor at best. I feel out of my league.

If you've counseled at all, then you've likely felt like Jim—confident in God's sufficient Word, concerned about your competency, and wondering whether your concern is wisdom based or fear based. This is why as biblical counselors we need to clarify the relationship between scriptural sufficiency and counselor competency.

A BRIEF INTRODUCTION TO THE SUFFICIENCY OF SCRIPTURE

To address this practical issue, it's important that we understand what the biblical counseling movement means by scriptural sufficiency.

In chapter 6, we introduced the Biblical Counseling Coalition's "Confessional Statement." The first of the twelve statements highlights scriptural sufficiency under the header "Biblical Counseling Must Be Anchored in Scripture." Here is the Coalition's succinct (379 words) summary of what sufficiency *is* and what it is *not*.

We believe that God's Word is authoritative, sufficient, and relevant (Isaiah 55:11; Matthew 4:4; Hebrews 4:12–13). The inspired and inerrant Scriptures, rightly interpreted and carefully applied, offer us God's comprehensive wisdom. We learn to understand who God is, who we are, the problems we face, how people change, and God's provision for that change in the Gospel (John 8:31–32; 10:10; 17:17). No other source of knowledge thoroughly equips us to counsel in ways that transform the human heart (Psalm 19:7–14; 2 Timothy 3:16–17; 2 Peter 1:3). Other systems of counseling aim for other goals and assume a different dynamic of change. The wisdom given by God in His Word is distinctive and robust. He comprehensively addresses the sin and suffering of all people in all situations.

Wise counseling is an insightful application of God's all-embracing truth to our complex lives (Romans 15:4; 1 Corinthians 10:6; Philippians 1:9–11). It does not merely collect proof-texts from the Bible. Wise counseling requires ongoing practical theological labor in order to understand Scripture, people, and situations (2 Timothy 2:15). We must continually develop our personal character, casewise understanding of people, and pastoral skills (Romans 15:14; Colossians 1:28–29).

When we say that Scripture is comprehensive in wisdom, we mean that the Bible makes sense of all things, not that it contains all the information people could ever know about all topics. God's common grace brings many good things to human life. However, common grace cannot save us from our struggles with sin or from the troubles that beset us. Common grace cannot sanctify or cure the soul of all that ails the human condition. We affirm that numerous sources (such as scientific research, organized observations about human behavior, those we counsel, reflection on our own life experience, literature, film, and history) can contribute to our knowledge of people, and many sources can contribute some relief for the troubles of life. However, none can constitute a comprehensive system of counseling principles and practices. When systems of thought and practice claim to prescribe a cure for the human condition, they compete with Christ (Colossians 2:1–15). Scripture alone teaches a perspective and way of looking at life by which we can think biblically about and critically evaluate information and actions from any source (Colossians 2:2–10; 2 Timothy 3:16–17).[1]

Thus, by "sufficiency of Scripture," biblical counselors mean that God's Word provides comprehensive wisdom for life in our broken world. While other resources can contribute to our understanding of life, only the Scriptures provide the overarching perspective by which we can critically evaluate all other potential sources of truth.

A BRIEF INTRODUCTION TO GROWING AS A COMPETENT BIBLICAL COUNSELOR

In Romans 15:14, Paul states that he's convinced that Christians have the capacity to become competent to comfort, encourage, confront, and disciple one another. When Paul used the word *convinced*, he chose a word that means an "internal conviction based upon external evidence."[2] A Christian who is becoming competent to counsel presents the following "4C" evidence or résumé from Romans 15:14 (NIV)—character, content, competence, and community:

- *Christlike Character*: We are growing in goodness—"full of goodness."

- *Biblical Content* (applied to life): We are growing in biblical wisdom—"filled with knowledge."
- *Counseling Competence*: We are growing in our ability to relate truth to life—"competent to instruct."
- *Christian Community*: We are growing in Christian one-another relational connection—"brothers," "one another."

Romans 15:14 served as a foundational verse for the modern biblical counseling movement. It has embedded within it markers that we can use to assess our growing competency. This is why a central hallmark of the modern biblical counseling movement has always been *ongoing equipping*. This equipping includes

- ongoing self-counsel and one-another mutual ministry to grow in Christlike character;
- ongoing reading, training, and education to grow in biblical content;
- ongoing supervised experience to grow in counseling competence, and
- ongoing connection to the larger body of Christ to grow within the context of Christian community.

As we read earlier from the "Confessional Statement,"

Wise counseling requires *ongoing* practical theological labor in order to understand Scripture, people, and situations (2 Timothy 2:15). We must *continually develop* our personal character, case-wise understanding of people, and pastoral skills (Romans 15:14; Colossians 1:28–29).

Further, no Christian is *self-sufficiently* competent to counsel. Our competency is dependent on Christ. Speaking of his ministry—after years of education and ministry experience—Paul states: "Not that we are competent in ourselves to claim anything for ourselves, but our competence comes from God. He has made us competent as ministers of a new covenant—not of the letter but of the Spirit; for the letter kills, but the Spirit gives life"

(2 Corinthians 3:5–6 NIV). We are *in*competent to counsel in our own strength and knowledge.

Additionally, no Christian is *independently* competent to counsel. We are one body made up of many parts (1 Corinthians 12:12–31). No part of the body can say to another part, "I don't need you!" (1 Corinthians 12:21). The Scriptures are sufficient; we are insufficient.

Christians can become increasingly competent to counsel through being equipped by the body of Christ, through humble dependence upon Christ, and through mutual ministry within the body of Christ.

TWO PRELIMINARY WAYS TO ASSESS OUR COMPETENCY

Let's return to Jim. By his own admission, he's a rookie counselor. If he read this chapter, he'd be quick to say, "I agree. I am not automatically, self-sufficiently, or independently competent to counsel this man who is hearing voices. Yet, I'm a rookie counselor who believes and trusts God's sufficient Word. So what should I do, Bob?"

Jim could start evaluating his competency to care for this individual by considering a few self-assessment questions. This will help him to see in which ways he is prepared to help his counselee and at what point he would be wise to reach out for additional assistance. I've provided two key self-assessment categories below:

Competency Assessment #1: "What's my level of overall growth and maturity in the 4Cs—Character, Content, Competence, Community—of Romans 15:14?"

Before we counsel others, we should be doing ongoing self-counsel and receiving feedback from others. If we are not actively growing in our personal discipleship and character development, we will be unfit to come alongside others to encourage them to take next steps in their own spiritual growth. Consider the following questions:

- To what degree am I growing in Christlike character, biblical content, counseling competency, and Christian community?
- What equipping and discipleship am I receiving to help me to grow in Christlike character, biblical content, counseling competency, and Christian community?
- What feedback am I receiving from others about my own progressive sanctification journey in Christlike character, biblical content, counseling competency, and Christian community?
- Am I at a stage in my Christian life where I'd be better off *receiving* formal counseling rather than *giving* informal one-another ministry or formal biblical counseling?

Competency Assessment #2: "What's my level of 4C equipping related to the particular issue I'm being asked to address?"

We may be in a healthy place of personal discipleship and growth and equipped to handle many types of counseling needs, but it is always wise to consider our level of experience and training, not to mention our own personal history, with particular struggles that are presented to us. We should consider the following questions when assessing our competency for the specific challenges our counselees bring to the table:

- *Character Assessment*: I'm being asked to help someone with anger issues. To what degree do I evidence growing Christlike maturity and progressive sanctification with this struggle?
- *Content Assessment*: I'm being asked to help someone with self-harm and cutting issues. What's my level of biblical knowledge, formal training, and personal research about this subject?

- *Competency Assessment*: I'm being asked to counsel someone dealing with past sexual abuse. What's my level of supervised experience with this sensitive issue?
- *Community Assessment*: I'm being asked to counsel someone hearing voices. Am I the best person in our church and in the surrounding Christian community to address this issue? Or are there others who are more qualified, and should I play more of a support role? If I am qualified to counsel, what additional help do I need to ensure that I minister well?

FIVE GUIDELINES TO ASSURE THAT COMPETENT HELP IS PROVIDED

Notice the precise wording in this header: *to assure that competent help is provided.* The united body of Christ through the power of Christ and the sufficiency of Scripture is competent to provide help for soul issues. However, no one individual is competent to provide all help for all issues.

We've been talking about Jim, the rookie counselor. Let's talk now about Bob, the experienced counselor. After almost four decades of counseling and almost three decades of equipping counselors, I do not see myself as automatically competent to counsel every person with every issue. For example, I've not had a great deal of education, nor do I have a great deal of experience counseling people regarding cutting and self-harm. So if someone came to me requesting my help with that issue, what might I do? What should you do? If we self-assess and determine that we don't have enough 4C qualification, how should we proceed?

Guideline #1: Consistently Involve a Comprehensive Body-of-Christ Team Approach

Regardless of whether I have sufficient training and experience with a given counseling issue, I should always follow a team approach. If a Christian is coming to a biblical counselor, they should be attending church, spending time in the Word and prayer, and participating in a small group, women's group, men's group, or Bible study. In addition, the potential counselee needs to have had a recent physical exam. Depending on the issue and the resources in the church and community, they might also be involved in an issue-specific recovery or growth group. They should be reading good Christian resources related to their issue. Ideally, they might benefit from having a family member or friend attend counseling with them as an advocate.

Counseling is one subset of the wider encouragement and discipleship ministry of the church. Counseling is not some "magic therapy hour" that negates the other 167 hours of the week. We always want to communicate that we are not the answer, Christ *is* the answer, and growth in grace is a church community journey.

Guideline #2: Prayerfully Ponder Whether the Wider Resources of the Body of Christ May Be Needed

The context of Romans 15:14 indicates that no one church is necessarily autonomously proficient to address every counseling issue. In chapter 16 of Romans, Paul addresses some of the many house churches in Rome. In a similar context, Paul leaves Timothy in Crete to appoint elders in every town (Titus 1:5). The New Testament assumes the interdependency of like-minded churches within a geographical area. Thus, it is totally appropriate for a church to utilize the expertise of other churches (and parachurch ministries) in the universal body of Christ. Biblical counselors (along with other leaders in the church) should seek to foster collaborative relationships with like-minded congregations in their vicinity in order to share encouragement, training, and other resources for ministering to people in need.

Guideline #3: Prayerfully Ponder Whether Resources outside the Church May Be Needed

The complexity and interrelated nature of many counseling issues require resources in addition to the church. We saw in chapters

6 and 8 the need for adjunctive resources—as the "Confessional Statement" of the Biblical Counseling Coalition wisely reminds us:

> We recognize the complexity of the relationship between the body and soul (Genesis 2:7). Because of this, we seek to remain sensitive to physical factors and organic issues that affect people's lives. In our desire to help people comprehensively, we seek to apply God's Word to people's lives amid bodily strengths and weaknesses. We encourage a thorough assessment and sound treatment for any suspected physical problems.
>
> We recognize the complexity of the connection between people and their social environment. Thus we seek to remain sensitive to the impact of suffering and of the great variety of significant social-cultural factors (1 Peter 3:8–22). In our desire to help people comprehensively, we seek to apply God's Word to people's lives amid both positive and negative social experiences. We encourage people to seek appropriate practical aid when their problems have a component that involves education, work life, finances, legal matters, criminality (either as a victim or a perpetrator), and other social matters.

Notice the encouragement for counselees (and counselors) to seek appropriate assistance outside the body of Christ—educational resources, financial services, legal assistance, etc.

Guideline #4: Have a Candid Conversation to Mutually Determine Your Next Steps, Potentially Refer to Others in the Body of Christ, Remain Part of a Team Approach

If we sense that a counselee's need might be outside our 4C competence, then we could candidly share with them our assessment of the best next steps. For instance, "The issue you're wrestling with is very important, and I want to be sure you have the best help possible. Though I've counseled for years, I'm not all that experienced in counseling people who struggle with cutting.

I know a biblical counselor within driving distance who has done so much work in this area that they've literally 'written the book on it.' Let's talk about whether I'm the best person to provide primary care for you or whether this other counselor might be a better fit. If so, I could come alongside and provide support."

Ideally you would still participate in the counseling as an advocate or counselor-in-training or eventually as a co-counselor. If not, the counselee could sign a release of information so you are kept informed by the other biblical counselor. You and the counselee could still meet informally for one-another ministry, encouragement, and discipleship as adjunctive help.

Guideline #5: Potentially Decide to Be the Primary Caregiver but Become Further Equipped and Be Supervised

There are other times when you and your counselee might have an honest conversation about your competency to counsel them, and you mutually decide that you will be their primary counselor. As always, a team approach is still the healthiest course, and now you add even more avenues for support for them and avenues of equipping and supervision for you. The following are examples.

- You counsel them under the supervision of a more experienced biblical counselor who reads your case notes, listens to your recorded counseling sessions, and provides ongoing mentoring.
- You do extensive research and study—exploring the Bible's teaching on the issue, reading biblical counseling books on the subject, and reading descriptive research on the topic.
- You attend specialized seminars, courses, and conferences to obtain further training.
- You learn from and together with your counselee. Early in my counseling ministry, a man asked for help dealing with past sexual abuse. I had my master's degree, I had specialized coursework in sexual abuse counseling,

but I had not counseled anyone who had been sexually abused. He still wanted me to counsel him. I asked him to teach me, to help me understand his heart, his suffering, his hurts, his walk with God.

IT'S ALL ABOUT HUMILITY

At the end of the day, it's all about humility. The Word is sufficient. We are incompetent in ourselves. Any competency in our counsel comes from Christ. Specific counseling competency requires ongoing 4C growth. And even the most competent biblical counselor must depend upon the comprehensive resources of the body of Christ. This well-rounded, Christ-dependent approach to ministry will keep our ministry focused on Jesus, the true source of all wisdom and knowledge.

ASSESSING OUR BIBLICAL COUNSELING

1. As biblical counselors, do we understand that while the Scriptures are sufficient for every soul issue, no individual counselor is competent for every soul issue?
2. As biblical counselors, are we committed to ongoing 4C growth in Christlike character, biblical content, counseling competency, and Christian community?
3. As biblical counselors, do we insist upon a comprehensive body of Christ approach where we humbly acknowledge our need for Christ and the body of Christ?
4. As biblical counselors, are we humbly willing to refer counselees to other, more experienced biblical counselors? Are we humbly willing to receive additional biblical supervision and equipping?

CONCLUSION
ASSESSING OUR BIBLICAL COUNSELING

WE CAN describe the personal ministry of the Word with two similar yet distinct words: *counsel, counseling*. This book has been less about *counsel*—the guidance we share, the information we give, or the advice and counsel we provide. That's all important, and there are many books that describe biblical truth related to a myriad of life issues.

This book has been more about *counseling*—the process, the journey, the relationship between the counselor and the counselee, *and* the mindset embedded behind the art of counseling. As I reflect on my supervision, my focus is often more on this issue of a counselor's thinking about the counseling process. When their mindsets about counseling change, then everything changes. I love seeing the light bulbs go on for supervisees. Someone might say, "Ah! So, emotions are not automatically evil! We can talk about them. We can enter them!"

And I love the freedom that counselors experience when their mindset changes about counseling. I enjoyed watching this in a recent biblical counseling training lab. On the last day of our weeklong lab, a mature male counselor with over three decades in the pastoral ministry shared with our group. With tears in his eyes, he said, "I feel like I've been given permission to do what I've always wanted to do as a counselor—empathize with people in their suffering and connect with people in their feelings. Somehow I had the wrong idea that counselors were to keep their distance, be aloof, talk about behavior, not address emotions, and race through suffering on the way to pointing out sin. Now my *counseling* seems

so much more alive, so much more real, so much like Paul in
1 Thessalonians 2:8 where he was delighted to give people both
God's Word and his very own soul!"

My prayer for you—and for me—is that your mindset about
counseling will be changed as you process this book. Let's put off
old, unbiblical mindsets about biblical counseling. Let's put on
new biblical mindsets about biblical counseling.

Because I'm a huge believer in the power of mindset change
to change our actual practice of counseling, this book has been
filled with few how-tos. It's not a methods book, as valuable as
those are.[1] I didn't want to "give you a fish"; I wanted to "teach
you to fish"—how to take the material in these ten chapters and
make them your own.

Throughout these materials, I've sought to teach you to fish
by highlighting the practical relevance of each of the ten counseling mistakes with the sections titled "Assessing Our Biblical
Counseling." As we bring this supervision in writing to a close,
I've collated those evaluations into a forty-question Biblical
Counselor's Self-Assessment Tool. As biblical counselors, we like
to speak of "self-counsel" and "progressive sanctification." We can
use these questions to do self-supervision so that we can progressively grow as biblical counselors.

A BIBLICAL COUNSELOR'S SELF-ASSESSMENT TOOL

Mistake #1: We Elevate Data Collection above Soul Connection

1. In our biblical counseling, would people say of us, "I feel
   like a soul to be heard, known, understood, and cared
   about"? Or would they say of us, "I feel like a specimen
   to be probed, dissected, examined, and diagnosed"?
2. In our biblical counseling, would people say of us, "She
   loves me like a tender, gentle mother. He loves me like an
   encouraging, comforting father"?

3. Would the people we counsel say of us, "They share Scripture and soul. They model intimacy and intensity. They relate like a family and a community"?

4. In our biblical counseling, how richly and compassionately are we empathizing with the situation and soul of our brothers and sisters in Christ?

Mistake #2: We Share God's Eternal Story before Listening to People's Earthly Story

5. In our biblical counseling, do we listen and pounce— preaching *at* people and doing so unwisely and prematurely? Or do we practice lingering listening to their whole story—taking the time to understand the person's situation and soul?

6. As biblical counselors, do we see our calling as journeying together with our counselees so that they can grasp how Christ's redemptive story intersects and invades their troubling story?

7. As biblical counselors, do we follow the model of the Holy Spirit—the Divine Counselor within us—who groans before and as he guides?

8. As biblical counselors, do we follow the model of Jesus— the Wonderful Counselor—by seeking to understand each individual and by tailoring our exploration of Scripture to their distinctive situation, story, and soul?

Mistake #3: We Talk *at* Counselees Rather Than Exploring Scripture *with* Counselees

9. Is our biblical counseling more directive (counselor as expert teller), more nondirective (counselees as experts about their own life), or more collaborative (counselor and counselee guided together by God's Word)?

10. As biblical counselors, which of the following is truer of our focus?

      a. Teaching/Telling Scripture→Give a Person a Fish→
      Make a Student of Yourself

      b. Exploring Scripture Together→Teach a Person to
      Fish→Make a Disciple of Christ

11. As biblical counselors, do we practice monologue counseling, dialogue counseling, or trialogue counseling—
where there are three people in our gospel conversation:
the counselor, the counselee, and the Divine Counselor
through God's Spirit and God's Word? Do we listen together to God's Word, discerning collaboratively how to
apply truth to life?

12. As biblical counselors, how could the 2 Samuel 13 sample trialogues impact our counseling practice, our counseling process, our counselor-counselee relationship, and
our counselee's life?

Mistake #4: We Target Sin but Diminish Suffering

13. Is our biblical counseling defective because it deals thoroughly with the sins we have committed but not with the
evils we have suffered?

14. As biblical counselors, do we sometimes have a one-track
mind that considers the seriousness of sin but neglects
the gravity of grinding affliction?

15. Do we see ourselves as *parakaletic* biblical counselors—
biblical soul caregivers who comfort, encourage, and
compassionately care for those facing suffering?

16. As biblical counselors, do we compassionately identify
with people in pain and direct them to Christ and the
body of Christ for comfort and healing hope?

Mistake #5: We Fail to Follow the Trinity's Model of Comforting Care

17. Do we counsel like God the Father? Do we sympathetically lament with others? Do others experience us as their

caring advocate, as their concerned protector, as their empathetic ally?

18. Do we counsel like God the Son? Do we sorrow with others? Do we grieve with others? Are we sympathetic toward and empathetic with others? Are we deeply moved by the suffering of others?

19. Do we counsel like God the Spirit? Are we consoling, comforting, and encouraging? Do we identify and groan with others?

20. Do we counsel like the Trinity? Does the comfort of the Father, Son, and Holy Spirit overflow from the Trinity to us and then spill over to our brothers and sisters?

Mistake #6: We View PeopleOne-Dimensionally Instead of Comprehensively

21. As biblical counselors, do we have a "pet" perspective of people—viewing them through one primary lens instead of viewing them comprehensively?

22. Do we believe that biblical counseling should focus on the full range of human nature created in the image of God (Genesis 1:26–28), comprehensively understanding counselees as *relational (spiritual, social, and self-aware), rational, volitional, emotional, and physical* beings?

23. As biblical counselors, are *we* growing in Christlike maturity as evidenced by the nine biblical categories in the Christlike Maturity Inventory?

24. As biblical counselors, do we seek to help our counselees grow in Christlike maturity as evidenced by the nine biblical categories in the Christlike Maturity Inventory?

Mistake #7: We Devalue Emotions Instead of Seeing Emotions as God's Idea

25. As biblical counselors, do we devalue and demean emotions, or do we see emotions as being of great value because they are God-designed aspects of the image of God?

26. How does it impact our biblical counseling when we realize that emotions were God's idea and that God specifically declares that our emotions are fearfully and wonderfully made?

27. In our biblical counseling, how well or how poorly are we using a biblical theology of our inner life? What we believe→about God and life→informs the direction we choose to pursue→and impacts our experiential/emotional response to our world.

28. In our biblical counseling, how well or how poorly are we using a practical theology of understanding our emotions as we enter, engage with, and enlighten our counselees?

Mistake #8: We Minimize the Complexity of the Body-Soul Interconnection

29. As soul physicians, does our emphasis on the soul morph into a sole focus on the soul that minimizes the complex interrelationship between the body and soul? Do we remain sensitive to physical factors and organic issues that affect people's lives? Do we encourage a thorough assessment and sound treatment for any suspected physical problems?

30. As soul physicians, do we understand and apply the Bible's Creation-Fall-Redemption teaching on the complex interrelationship of the body and soul—as designed by God, depraved by sin, and saved by grace?

31. As soul physicians, do we seek to understand the impact of the body on our counselee's soul? Do we seek to understand the soul's impact on our counselee's body?

32. Like Luther, as physicians of the soul, do we avoid a materialistic worldview that assumes every issue is exclusively biologically based? And do we avoid a spiritualistic worldview that assumes every issue is exclusively soul-based?

Mistake #9: We Maximize Sin while Minimizing Grace

33. Which do we emphasize as biblical counselors: sin or grace? In our concern for confronting sin, do we sometimes inadvertently become sin-sniffers, idol-spotters, and sin-maximizers? Or as we confront sin, do we consciously communicate Christ's superabounding, amazing, infinite grace?

34. As biblical counselors, are we like Paul in Romans 5:20, reminding one another that where sin abounds, grace superabounds?

35. As biblical counselors, are we like the Puritans—able to load the conscience with guilt *and* to lighten the conscience with grace? Like Luther, are we dispensers of Christ's gospel of grace?

36. As biblical counselors, are we loving ambassadors of reconciliation who seek to share that "it's horrible to sin, but it's wonderful to be forgiven"?

Mistake #10: We Confuse the Sufficiency of Scripture with the Competency of the Counselor

37. As biblical counselors, do we understand that while the Scriptures are sufficient for every soul issue, no individual counselor is competent for every soul issue?

38. As biblical counselors, are we committed to ongoing 4C growth in Christlike character, biblical content, counseling competency, and Christian community?

39. As biblical counselors, do we insist upon a comprehensive body of Christ approach where we humbly acknowledge our need for Christ and the body of Christ?

40. As biblical counselors, are we humbly willing to refer counselees to other more experienced biblical counselors? Are we humbly willing to receive additional biblical supervision and equipping?

BIBLIOGRAPHY

Albert, Octavia, ed. *The House of Bondage: Or Charlotte Brooks and Other Slaves*. Reprint edition. New York: Oxford University Press, 1988.

Berger, Daniel. *Rethinking Depression: Not a Sickness Not a Sin*. Taylors, SC: Alethia International Publications, 2019.

Biblical Counseling Coalition. "Confessional Statement." Accessed on December 1, 2020 at http://biblicalcounselingcoalition. org/about/confessional-statement/.

Bonhoeffer, Dietrich. *Life Together: The Classic Exploration of Christian in Community*. New York: Harper One, 2009.

Clebsch, William, and Charles Jaekle. *Pastoral Care in Historical Perspective: An Essay with Exhibits*. New York: Prentice Hall, 1964.

Emlet, Michael R. *Descriptions and Prescriptions: A Biblical Perspective on Psychiatric Diagnoses and Medications*. Greensboro, NC: New Growth Press, 2017.

———. "Listening to Prozac . . . and to the Scriptures: A Primer on Psychoactive Medications." *The Journal of Biblical Counseling* 26, no. 1 (2012): 11–22.

Frances, Allen. *Saving Normal: An Insider's Revolt against Out-of-Control Psychiatric Diagnosis, DSM-5, Big Pharma, and the Medicalization of Ordinary Life*. New York: William Morrow, 2014.

Hendrickson, Laura. "The Complex Mind/Body Connection." In *Christ-Centered Biblical Counseling: Changing Lives with God's Changeless Truth*, edited by Bob Kellemen and Steve Viars. Rev. ed. Eugene, OR: Harvest House, 2021.

Hodges, Charles. *Good Mood Bad Mood: Help and Hope for Depression and Bi-Polar Disorder.* Wapwallopen, PA: Shepherd Press, 2013.

Kellemen, Bob. *Counseling Under the Cross: How Martin Luther Applied the Gospel to Daily Life.* Greensboro, NC: New Growth Press, 2017.

———. *Grief: Walking with Jesus.* Phillipsburg, NJ: P&R, 2018.

Kellemen, Bob, and Kevin Carson, eds. *Biblical Counseling and the Church: God's Care through God's People.* Grand Rapids, MI: Zondervan, 2015.

Kellemen, Bob and Jeff Forrey, eds. *Scripture and Counseling: God's Word for Life in a Broken World.* Grand Rapids, MI: Zondervan, 2014.

Kellemen, Robert. *Anxiety: Anatomy and Cure.* Phillipsburg, NJ: P&R, 2012.

———. *God's Healing for Life's Losses: How to Find Hope When You're Hurting.* Winona Lake, IN: BMH, 2010.

———. *Gospel-Centered Counseling: How Christ Changes Lives.* Grand Rapids, MI: Zondervan, 2015.

———. *Gospel-Centered Family Counseling: An Equipping Guide for Pastors and Counselors.* Grand Rapids, MI: Baker, 2020.

———. *Gospel-Centered Marriage Counseling: An Equipping Guide for Pastors and Counselors.* Grand Rapids, MI: Baker, 2020.

———. *Gospel Conversations: How to Care Like Christ.* Grand Rapids, MI: Zondervan, 2014.

———. *Sexual Abuse: Beauty for Ashes.* Phillipsburg, NJ: P&R, 2013.

———. *What Does the Bible Teach About Our Emotions? Learning the ABCs of Emotional Intelligence?* Accessed on December 1, 2020 at http://bit.ly/EmotionsABCs.

Kellemen, Robert W., and Karole Edwards. *Beyond the Suffering: Embracing the Legacy of African American Soul Care and Spiritual Direction.* Grand Rapids, MI: Baker, 2007.

Lake, Frank. *Clinical Theology: A Theological and Psychiatric Basis to Clinical Pastoral Care*. London: Darton, Longman, & Todd, 1966.

Luther, Martin. *The Babylonian Captivity of the Church in Three Treatises*. Translated by P. Smith. Philadelphia: Muhlenberg, 1531/1947.

———. *Commentary on Galatians*. Translated by P. S. Watson. Grand Rapids: Fleming H. Revell, 1535/1988.

———. "Table Talk." In *Luther's Works*. Vol. 54, edited and translated by T. T. Tappert. Philadelphia: Fortress, 1967.

Nebe, August, ed. *Luther as Spiritual Adviser*. Translated by C. H. Hays. Philadelphia: Lutheran Publication Society, 1894.

Pierre, Jeremy. *The Dynamic Heart in Daily Life: Connecting Christ to Human Experience*. Greensboro, NC: New Growth Press, 2016.

Piper, John. *The Pleasures of God: Meditations on God's Delight in Being God*. Colorado Springs: Multnomah, 2000.

Powlison, David. "Idols of the Heart and 'Vanity Fair.'" *Journal of Biblical Counseling* 13, no. 2 (Winter 1995): 35–50.

Shorter, Edward. *How Everyone Became Depressed: The Rise and Fall of the Nervous Breakdown*. New York: Oxford University Press, 2013.

Smith, Preserved. *The Life and Letters of Martin Luther*. New York: Barnes and Noble, 1911.

Somerville, Robert. *If I'm a Christian, Why Am I Depressed?* Maitland, FL: Xulon, 2014.

Viars, Steve. "'Brian'" and Obsessive-Compulsive Disorder." In *Counseling the Hard Cases*, edited by Stuart Scott and Heath Lambert. Nashville: B&H Academics, 2012.

Welch, Edward T. *Blame It on the Brain?: Distinguishing Chemical Imbalances, Brain Disorders, and Disobedience*. Phillipsburg, NJ: P&R, 1998.

Wolff, Hans. *Anthropology of the Old Testament*. London: SCM Press, 1974.

ENDNOTES

Introduction

1. Robert W. Kellemen, *Gospel-Centered Counseling* (Grand Rapids, MI: Zondervan, 2014).

2. Robert W. Kellemen, *Gospel Conversations: How to Care Like Christ* (Grand Rapids, MI: Zondervan, 2015).

Mistake #1

1. Octavia Albert, *The House of Bondage* (New York: Oxford University Press, reprint 1988), 2.

2. Albert, 15.

3. Albert, 28–29.

Mistake #2

1. Dietrich Bonhoeffer, *Life Together: The Classic Exploration of Christian in Community* (HarperOne: New York, 2009) 99.

2. Bonhoeffer, 97–98.

3. See Kellemen, *Gospel-Centered Counseling* for a training manual on how to relate God's story to people's life story.

Mistake #3

1. William A. Clebsch and Charles R. Jaekle, *Pastoral Care in Historical Perspective* (Prentice Hall: New York, 1964), 1–41.

2. In *Gospel Conversations*, I comprehensively develop this concept of trialogues, providing hundreds of sample trialogues to equip biblical counselors for engaging in scriptural explorations and spiritual conversations with counselees.

3. I develop Ashley's story and a biblical counseling response in Kellemen, *Sexual Abuse: Beauty for Ashes* (Phillipsburg, NJ: P&R, 2013).

Mistake #4

1. Frank Lake, *Clinical Theology* (London: Darton, Longman & Todd, 1966), 25.

2. Lake, 25.

Mistake #6

1. David Powlison, "Idols of the Heart and 'Vanity Fair,'" *Journal of Biblical Counseling* 13, no. 2 (Winter 1995): 35–50.

2. Biblical Counseling Coalition, "Confessional Statement," accessed December 1, 2020, https://www.biblicalcounselingcoalition.org/confessional-statement/.

3. Kellemen, *Gospel-Centered Counseling.*

Mistake #7

1. Kellemen, *What Does the Bible Teach About Our Emotions? Learning the ABCs of Emotional Intelligence*, accessed December 1, 2020, http://bit.ly/EmotionsABCs.

2. John Piper, *The Pleasures of God: Meditations on God's Delight in Being God* (Colorado Springs: Multnomah, 2000) 72.

3. Hans Wolff, *Anthropology of the Old Testament* (London: SCM Press, 1974).

4. Kellemen, *What Does the Bible Teach About Our Emotions?.*

Mistake #8

1. Biblical Counseling Coalition, "Confessional Statement."

2. See Laura Hendrickson, "The Complex Mind/Body Connection," *Christ-Centered Biblical Counseling: Changing Lives with God's Changeless Truth*, rev. ed., eds. Bob Kellemen and Steve Viars (Eugene, OR: Harvest House, 2021), 409–22.

3. Hendrickson, 409–22.

4. Hendrickson, 409–22.

5. Daniel Berger, *Rethinking Depression* (Taylors, SC: Alethia International Publications, 2019); Michael R. Emlet, *Descriptions and Prescriptions* (Greensboro, NC: New Growth Press, 2017); Michael R. Emlet, "Listening to Prozac . . . and to the Scriptures: A Primer on Psychoactive Medications" *Journal of Biblical Counseling* 26, no. 1 (2012); Hendrickson, "The Complex Mind/Body Connection"; Charles Hodges, *Good Mood Bad Mood* (Wapwallopen, PA: Shepherd Press, 2013); Robert Somerville, *If I'm a Christian, Why Am I Depressed?* (Maitland, FL: Xulon Press); and Edward T. Welch, *Blame It on the Brain?* (Phillipsburg, NJ: P&R, 1998).

6. Hendrickson, "The Complex Mind/Body Connection," 418.

7. See Allen Frances, *Saving Normal* (New York: William Morrow, 2014); Edward Shorter, *How Everyone Became Depressed* (New York: Oxford University Press, 2013).

8. For a nuanced perspective on the current state of psychotropic interventions, see Hodges, *Good Mood Bad Mood.*

9. Hendrickson, "The Complex Mind/Body Connection," 415.

10. Martin Luther, *Luther's Works*, vol. 53, 54, ed. and trans. T. T. Tappert (Philadelphia: Fortress, 1967).

11. *Luther's Works*, 53.

12. *Luther's Works*, 53–54.

13. Preserved Smith, *The Life and Letters of Martin Luther* (New York: Barnes and Noble, 1911), 402.

14. Smith, 402.

15. Emlet, "Listening to Prozac . . . and to the Scriptures," 21.

Mistake #9

1. August Nebe, ed., *Luther as Spiritual Adviser*, trans. C. H. Hays (Philadelphia: Lutheran Publication Society, 1894), 181.

2. Martin Luther, *The Babylonian Captivity of the Church in Three Treatises*, trans. P. Smith (Philadelphia: Muhlenberg, 1947), 201.

3. Martin Luther, *Commentary on Galatians*, trans. P. S. Watson (Grand Rapids, MI: Fleming H. Revell, 1988), 70.

4. Luther, *Commentary on Galatians*, 314.

Mistake #10

1. Biblical Counseling Coalition, "Confessional Statement."

2. For a fuller discussion of Romans 15:14 and the "4Cs" of counselor competence, see, Kellemen, *Gospel Conversations*, 77–94.

Conclusion

1. For three comprehensive biblical counseling method books, see my works: *Gospel Conversations*; *Gospel-Centered Marriage Counseling: An Equipping Guide for Pastors and Counselors* (Grand Rapids, MI: Baker Books, 2020); and *Gospel-Centered Family Counseling: An Equipping Guide for Pastors and Counselors* (Grand Rapids: Baker Books, 2020).